Wisdom for Thinkers

CURRENT AND FORTHCOMING TITLES

ACADEMIC INTRODUCTIONS
FOR BEGINNERS

AVAILABLE

VOLUME ONE WISDOM FOR THINKERS: AN INTRODUCTION TO
            CHRISTIAN PHILOSOPHY

VOLUME TWO POWER IN SERVICE: AN INTRODUCTION TO
            CHRISTIAN POLITICAL THOUGHT

TO BE RELEASED IN 2014

VOLUME THREE THINKING GOD'S THOUGHTS: AN INTRODUCTION TO
            CHRISTIAN THEOLOGY

VOLUME FOUR SEARCHING THE SOUL: AN INTRODUCTION TO
            CHRISTIAN PSYCHOLOGY

TO BE RELEASED IN 2015

VOLUME FIVE LIFE IS BEAUTIFUL: AN INTRODUCTION TO
            CHRISTIAN BIOLOGY

VOLUME SIX   PROBING THE PAST: AN INTRODUCTION TO
            CHRISTIAN HISTORICAL SCIENCE

WISDOM
FOR
THINKERS

An Introduction to Christian Philosophy

Willem J. Ouweneel

PAIDEIA PRESS
2014

A Publication of the
REFORMATIONAL PUBLISHING PROJECT
www.reformationalpublishingproject.com
and
PAIDEIA PRESS,
P. O. Box 500,
Jordan Station,
Ontario, Canada, L0R 1S0

© PAIDEIA PRESS 2014

ISBN 978-0-88815-226-8

Cover design and layout: Bill Muir

Printed in the United States of America

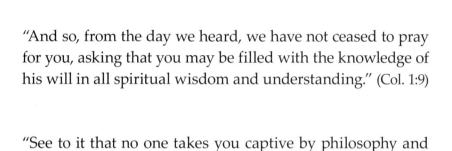

"And so, from the day we heard, we have not ceased to pray for you, asking that you may be filled with the knowledge of his will in all spiritual wisdom and understanding." (Col. 1:9)

"See to it that no one takes you captive by philosophy and empty deceit, according to human tradition, according to the elemental spirits of the world, and not according to Crist."

(Col. 2:8)

CONTENTS

ABOUT THE AUTHOR   xii

FOREWORD   xiii

CHAPTER 1   INTRODUCTION TO THIS INTRODUCTION   1
            "WHAT IS" QUESTIONS   1
            THEORIES ARE USEFUL   2
            THE BASIC QUESTIONS   3
            PHILOSOPHY IS UNAVOIDABLE   4
            TWO "LEGS"   5
            OUR WORLDVIEW   6
            PHILOSOPHIES ARE NOT WORLDVIEWS   7
            FAITH AND BELIEFS   8
            RELIGION   10
            CHRISTIAN PHILOSOPHY   12
            TRUE AND FALSE RELIGION   14
            QUESTIONS FOR REVIEW   16

CHAPTER 2   KNOWLEDGE AND WISDOM   17
            PHILOSOPHY AND SCIENCE   17
            TWO ROOTS   19
            EARLY CHRISTIANITY AND THE MIDDLE AGES   21
            THE MODERN AGE   23
            THE TWENTIETH CENTURY   25
            REFORMATIONAL PHILOSOPHY   26
            RELIGIOUS GROUND-MOTIVES (1)   27
            MODERN PHILOSOPHICAL SCHOOLS   28
            FAITH, REASON, FEELING   29
            SOME SPECIAL POINTS   32
            RELIGIOUS GROUND-MOTIVES (2)   34
            QUESTIONS FOR REVIEW   36

CHAPTER 3   A CHRISTIAN VIEW OF COSMIC REALITY   39
            THE COHERENCE OF THE SPECIAL SCIENCES   39
            HUMANITIES   41
            SEQUENTIAL ORDER AND ARRANGEMENT   43
            PHENOMENA AND ASPECTS   44
            SIXTEEN MODAL ASPECTS?   46
            IDOLATRY   48
            PROPERTIES OF MODAL ASPECTS   51
            HISTORICAL NOTE   52
            FINALLY: TIME   53
            TEMPORAL MODALITIES   54
            QUESTIONS FOR REVIEW   57

CHAPTER 4   COSMIC REALITY AND GOD'S LAW   59
            LAW-SPHERES   59
            NATURAL LAWS AND NORMS   61
            DISCOVERING NORMS AND LAWS   64
            SUBJECT-FUNCTIONS   65
            OBJECT-FUNCTIONS   67
            FOUR ADDITIONAL REMARKS   68
            CHRISTIAN MEANING   69
            KERNELS   71
            ANALOGIES   72
            THE LAW AS BOUNDARY   74
            STRUCTURE AND DIRECTION   76
            SIN AND REDEMPTION   78
            QUESTIONS FOR REVIEW   79

CHAPTER 5   A CHRISTIAN VIEW OF ENTITIES   81
            KINDS OF ENTITIES   82
            NATURE AND CULTURE   84
            THE NOTION OF THE IDIONOMY   86
            ENCAPSIS   88
            THE STRUCTURE OF A PLANT   90
            THE STRUCTURE OF A LOWER ANIMAL   92
            THE STRUCTURE OF A HIGHER ANIMAL   93
            QUESTIONS FOR REVIEW   95

CHAPTER 6   A CHRISTIAN ANTHROPOLOGY   **97**
             THE FIRST HUMAN IDIONOMY   97
             THE NEXT THREE HUMAN IDIONOMIES   98
             MAN'S SPIRITIVE IDIONOMY   100
             MAN'S EGO   102
             DICHOTOMY AND TRICHOTOMY   103
             THE END OF DUALISM   105
             A NEW APPROACH   106
             MARRIAGE AND FAMILY   108
             THE STATE   110
             THE CHURCH   112
             OTHER SOCIETAL RELATIONSHIPS   113
             QUESTIONS FOR REVIEW   115

CHAPTER 7   A PHILOSOPHY OF SCIENCE   **117**
             SCIENTISM   117
             BIBLIOSCIENTISM   118
             CRITICAL, WELL-FOUNDED KNOWLEDGE   119
             SYSTEMATIC, COHERENT KNOWLEDGE   120
             DETACHED, UNCONCERNED KNOWLEDGE   122
             ANALYTICAL, ABSTRACT KNOWLEDGE   123
             OBJECTIVE, REPRODUCIBLE KNOWLEDGE   124
             CRITERIA OF SCIENCE   125
             SCIENCE AND ABSTRACTION   126
             PRACTICAL OBSERVATION   128
             "LADEN" SENSATIONS   130
             PRACTICAL VERSUS THEORETICAL OBSERVATIONS   131
             THEORETICAL OBSERVATIONS   132
             THEORETICAL ENTITIES AND LAWS   133
             QUESTIONS FOR REVIEW   135

CHAPTER 8   SCIENCE AND WORLDVIEWS   **137**
             THE SENSITIVE ASPECT   137
             THE LOGICAL ASPECT   138
             THE FORMATIVE ASPECT   139
             THE SOCIAL ASPECT   140
             THE PISTICAL ASPECT   142
             "THE" WESTERN WORLDVIEW   143

"SCIENTIFIC" WORLDVIEWS   145
NATURALISM   146
CONSEQUENCES WITHIN SCIENCE   147
A CHRISTIAN WORLDVIEW   149
QUESTIONS FOR REVIEW   153

CHAPTER 9   PHILOSOPHY AND THEOLOGY   155
             THEOLOGICAL AND PHILOSOPHICAL GUILT   155
             SOME GENERAL STATEMENTS   156
             PHILOSOPHICAL PREMISES FOR THEOLOGY   157
             RATIONALISM VERSUS IRRATIONALISM   160
             NO THEOLOGY WITHOUT PHILOSOPHY   161
             THE ORIGIN OF THEOLOGY'S PHILOSOPHICAL
             PREMISES   163
             MISUNDERSTANDINGS   165
             GOOD AND BAD THEOLOGY/PHILOSOPHY   166
             THE HERMENEUTICAL CIRCLE   167
             FOREIGN ELEMENTS IN CHRISTIAN PHILOSOPHY? 169
             QUESTIONS FOR REVIEW   171

CHAPTER 10   TRUTH   173
             IS CHRISTIAN PHILOSOPHY TRUE?   174
             SCIENCE AND TRUTH   175
             GOD TEACHES THE FARMER   176
             THEORIES OF TRUTH   178
             CORRESPONDENCE   179
             SCIENTIFIC REALISM   180
             INSTRUMENTALISM   182
             CRITICAL REALISM   183
             THEORETICAL TRUTH   184
             PARTIAL TRUTH   187
             THE A PRIORI ELEMENTS OF TRUTH   189
             QUESTIONS FOR REVIEW   191

CONCISE BIBLIOGRAPHY   193

INDEXES   197

About the Author

Willem J. Ouweneel (b. 1944) earned his Ph.D. in biology at the University of Utrecht (The Netherlands, 1970), his Ph.D. in philosophy at the Free University in Amsterdam (The Netherlands, 1986), and his Ph.D. in theology at the University of the Orange Free State in Bloemfontein (Republic of South Africa, 1993). Among many other things, he has been Professor of the Philosophy of Science for the Natural Sciences at the University for Christian Higher Education in Potchefstroom (Republic of South Africa, 1990-1998), and Professor of Philosophy and Systematic Theology at the Evangelical Theological Faculty in Leuven (Belgium, 1995-2014). He is a prolific writer (mainly in Dutch), and has preached in more than thirty countries.

FOREWORD

The publisher of this book kindly invited me to write this introduction to Christian philosophy. He expressly asked me to write not a scholarly book, with many learned footnotes and an extensive bibliography, but a "simple" introduction that could appeal to students in the last years of high school, or the first years of college or university.

I have hesitantly accepted this invitation, because I could think of others who might have done a better job, and because writing a relatively easy book is quite difficult. I am not sure at all whether I have managed to properly fulfill my task; in reading again what I have written, I find certain passages that are quite complicated, particularly in the later chapters. Actually, that is no wonder, because the deeper we get into our subject, the more demanding it inevitably will become for readers. So, dear student, find out how far you will get in this book!

One technical matter requires mention. The English Bible translation being used in this book is the English Standard Version, unless otherwise noted.

I do hope that students, and other interested readers as well, will pick up the gist of what I want to say. There is something called "Christian philosophy," and it is not only highly fascinating, but also extremely useful for everyone who is interested in science in the broadest sense, including "even" the science of theology.

Willem J. Ouweneel
Zeist (The Netherlands)
Autumn 2013

Chapter One

INTRODUCTION
TO THIS INTRODUCTION

"What Is" Questions

This book is supposed to be an introduction to Christian philosophy. Such an introduction must itself first be introduced. We will immediately need to answer some vital introductory questions. The first one, of course, is: What is philosophy? Many people today use the term in a rather sloppy way. They speak of the "philosophy" of this business or of that company, the "philosophy" of the new government, etc.. They mean only the basic ideas, starting-points, and policies of this business or that government, and these are very practical matters. We, however, will speak of philosophy as a *science*, a theoretical enterprise—indeed, as the mother of all sciences.

In this book, I am using the word *science* in a very broad sense, including not just the natural sciences but also the humanities like psychology, sociology, economics, and even theology. "Science," in the broad way in which I am using the word, is what the Germans and the Dutch call *Wissenschaft* and *wetenschap*, respectively.

The second question we will have to answer is: What is *Christian* philosophy? We can easily imagine Christians doing philosophy, just as Christians can do house building, gardening, or stamp collecting. But is there a typically Christian way of building houses, gardening, or collecting stamps? In the same vein, one may wonder whether there is a typically Christian way of doing philosophy. "Christian philosophy" may sound just as crazy as Christian mathematics or Christian biology. All the same, in this book I am going to defend this very thesis: There *is* something like *Christian* philosophy—just as there is, for that matter, a Christian philosophy of mathematics, and a Christian philosophy of biology, as we will see.

1

Theories are Useful

The third question that may arise immediately is this: Why does it matter? For instance, why does it matter whether there is a Christian philosophy or not? Many people are very practically minded. They like to *do* things; for instance, engineers like to build roads or bridges, and psychologists like to help people with emotional and mental problems. In general, such scientists do not like theoretical matters very much, because the latter seem far removed from the challenges of daily life. In particular, Christians may think they are more "useful" if they do certain things for society instead of dabbling in theoretical questions that seem to be "useful" only for some boring scholars stuck in their offices.

I hope to show to you that this is a big mistake. Engineers have been studying engineering in order to be able to build bridges, machines, and many other things, and psychologists have been studying psychology in order to be able to help people with their mental problems. But did such scientists never wonder why these engineering sciences are called *science*, or why psychology is called *science*? What is so scientific about these sciences? In what essential way do they differ from the practical insights of many clever people who know how to build things, or how to help people, without ever having studied these *sciences*? Are engineering or psychology called sciences simply because they are more complex, more sophisticated, than these practical insights? Is *science* just a matter of complexity and sophistication? What makes science to be *science*? You may be astonished to hear that this is basically not a physical, or psychological, or cultural, or mathematical, or technical question at all, but a *philosophical* question.

One part of philosophy is called *philosophy of science* (the Germans and the Dutch have one word for this: *Wissenschaftslehre* and *wetenschapsleer*, respectively). You might even call it the "science of sciences," not in the sense of the "best" or "highest" science, but in the sense of the science *about* sciences—the science that answers questions like: What makes science to be science? In what way does a theoretical enterprise as science differ from practical knowledge? How can we distinguish between good science and bad science? What is the methodology of genuine science? Because science is indeed a theoretical enterprise, some people call the philosophy of science a *theory of theories*. It is a theory about how people form scientific theories, in other words, a theory about how people do science.

The Basic Questions

If you have studied, or are studying, engineering or psychology, you might at least be interested in the question of what kind of thing you actually have been doing so far. And, as I said, perhaps to your surprise, this turns out to be a philosophical question. There are many more philosophical questions that can be asked with respect to engineering or psychology. (And remember, engineering and psychology are only examples; you could ask similar questions with respect to *all* sciences.) Engineering is intertwined with mathematics and physics, on the one hand, and with cultural sciences on the other, for building things is a cultural matter, as we will see in chapter 4. Therefore, it is founded on both natural philosophy and cultural philosophy. Psychology has to do with the domain of the human mind, and is therefore founded on what we call philosophical anthropology, that is, the philosophy about what and who is Man.

Now, if you want to do natural sciences, cultural sciences, and human sciences, and you want to do them properly, you cannot avoid the basic "what is" questions. What *is* nature? (Or if we want to be tongue in cheek: what is the nature of nature?) What *is* culture? What *is* Man? Everyone who studies (aspects of) nature, culture, or Man, and wants to do it thoroughly, will sooner or later bump into such questions. Understandably so, for how can you do psychology without having some basic ideas about what kind of entity Man is, somewhere in the back of your mind?

Talking of minds, how can you be occupied with human minds without having some (vague) ideas, in the back of your mind, of what minds *are*? Perhaps you hardly *think* about such questions— because you are such a practical person, remember?—but these vague ideas must be there somewhere. You can hardly do without them. In a similar way, people doing (one of the) natural sciences must have some (vague) idea about what nature is. People doing (one of the) cultural sciences must have some (vague) idea about what culture is, no matter how inaccurate or how subconscious.

Philosophy is Unavoidable

Again, it is of the utmost importance to understand that all such questions—What is nature? What is culture? What is Man?—and all questions derived from them, are by definition *philosophical* questions. I cannot help it, but that is what they are. Perhaps you think that the question "What is psychology?" is a psychological question. That is a mistake, and I can easily demonstrate that. Psychological questions are usually answered by psychological observations and psychological experiments. But there is no psychological observation and no psychological experiment that ever will, or is ever even able to, answer the question "What is psychology?"

Let me use a simple illustration. Cameras can make pictures of their surroundings, but with a camera you cannot make a picture of its own interior; you would need some other camera for that. In the same way, psychology can explain certain psychical phenomena, but it cannot explain its own nature; you need some other science for that. That science is called the "disciplinary (or special) philosophy" of psychology. (German: *Fachphilosophie*; Dutch: *vakfilosofie*). It is that part of psychology that handles questions like: What is psychology? What makes psychology a science? What are the starting-points and methods of psychology? How can we distinguish good psychology from bad psychology? How does psychology relate to other *humanities* on the one hand, such as linguistics, historiography, sociology, and economics, and to the natural sciences on the other hand, especially biology?

Every science, from mathematics to theology, has to deal with similar basic questions. These questions are handled in that part of philosophy that belongs to it, ranging from the special philosophy (*Fachphilosophie*) of mathematics to the special philosophy (*Fachphilosophie*) of theology.

To summarize: if psychology is the science that studies psychical phenomena, we have to answer at least two questions right away. First, what is science? (How is scientific psychology to be distinguished from non-academic "psychology?") The answer is to be found in the *philosophy of science* (*Wissenschaftslehre*). Secondly, what are psychical phenomena? How are they to be distinguished from, for instance, physical, physiological, or social phenomena? The answer is to be found in the *special philosophy* of psychology.

In both respects, we have to do with philosophical questions. Are you beginning to see that, if you really want to study something in a scientific way, you cannot possibly avoid philosophical questions?

Two "Legs"

Let's now take another step. Science is a specific (theoretical) form of knowledge. Therefore, the philosophy of science is part of the wider field of what we call *epistemology*, that is, the philosophy of knowledge (German: *Erkenntnislehre* or *Erkenntnistheorie*; Dutch: *kennisleer* or *kennistheorie*). This is that part of philosophy that tries to answer questions like: What is knowledge? How can we know that we know something? What are the criteria for true knowledge? In what way do we acquire knowledge? Epistemology is the one "leg" on which philosophy stands.

The other "leg" is *ontology*, that is, the philosophy of *being*, the philosophy of all things that *are*, or simply, of all things that exist, the philosophy of the whole of cosmic reality. This is that part of philosophy that tries to answer questions like: What is *being*? What are the things that *are*? What is the nature of reality? How do the various parts within reality hang together? Can reality be reduced to some basic principle that can explain all the other aspects of it? (For example, "Everything is basically physical or material," or, "Everything is basically psychical or spiritual," or, "The whole of culture can be explained from economic relationships," etc.) Also, what is the origin of reality? And is there a purpose in reality? Where is the cosmos going?

Some people prefer the term *metaphysics* (the study of what lies behind the physical world) to *ontology*. Others prefer the term (philosophical) *cosmology*, because philosophy does not study *all* that *is*—the world of God, the angels, and the heavens lies outside its analysis—but only cosmic reality. No matter what terms one uses, these are the two "legs" of philosophy: the philosophy of knowledge, and the philosophy of (cosmic) reality. Of course, the two are closely related. True knowledge is always intended knowledge about reality. If there were no knowledge, reality might be there without us knowing anything about it. And conversely, if there were no reality, there would be nothing to know anything about.

Some, like the great German philosopher, Immanuel Kant, wanted to add a third "leg," namely, ethics, but I think this is incorrect; I will show why I see ethics as one of the many special sciences (German: *Fachwissenschaften*; Dutch: *vakwetenschappen*), or more specifically, as one of the many *humanities* (German: *Menschwissenschaften*; Dutch: *menswetenschappen*), just like psychology, sociology, economics, aesthetics, and theology.

I am now ready to give you a preliminary answer to the very first question I asked at the beginning of this chapter: What is philosophy? *Philosophy is that foundational science—the "science of sciences"—that endeavors to answer the most basic and vital questions about all our knowing and being, or about knowledge and reality.* It is a *totality* science, because it does not look at the various parts of reality separately, as do the special sciences, but tries to get the total picture. The (always preliminary) answers to the questions I mentioned consciously or unconsciously underlie all our thinking, particularly our theoretical, or our scientific, thinking. There is no really scientific thinking without some philosophical basis, and wise scientists will try to account for this basis.

Our Worldview

Let's take another step. If every science is founded upon philosophy as the "science of sciences," then on what science is philosophy founded? That sounds a bit like the question: If all things were created by God, then by what was God created? The answer is: If something had created God, then that something would in fact be God. Similarly, philosophy is not rooted in some "higher," or if you like, "deeper" science, simply because philosophy is itself, by definition, the "highest" or "deepest" science. If philosophy were rooted in some "higher" science, then that "higher science" would by definition be philosophy.

That does not mean that philosophy has no foundation. It has. But that foundation is not philosophical or scientific in nature. You might call it our (pre-philosophical or pre-scientific or pre-theoretical) *worldview* (German: *Weltanschauung*; Dutch: *wereldbeschouwing*). A worldview is a (frequently non-articulated) set of ideas and principles concerning the world in which we live, the nature, the origin, and the purpose (or lack of purpose) of this world, etc. (see especially chapter 8). It is always intertwined with a *view of life* (German: *Lebensanschauung*; Dutch: *levensbeschouwing*), that is, a (frequently non-articulated) set of ideas and principles concerning the meaning and value (or lack of meaning and value) of human life, the nature, the origin, and the purpose (or lack of purpose) of that life, etc. Our view of the world and our view of life are interconnected: it is this world in which we live and to which we relate.

Later I will try to show that there is no such thing as a purely objective, unbiased, unprejudiced philosophy, that is, a philosophy without even the tiniest pre-conceived ideas about the (possible) meaning of the world and of human life. In other words, there is no true philosophy without some worldview that underlies it. There are many people who have a worldview while not having anything that deserves the name "philosophy." But in my opinion, the reverse is not quite possible: you cannot have your own philosophy without some sort of a preceding worldview.

Philosophies Are Not Worldviews

Let me add an important point here. In practice, in many cases there are seemingly not many differences between philosophies and worldviews. Much of what is called "philosophy" today has little to do with actual philosophy, like cosmology and epistemology, but is more practical wisdom. This is largely because, for many people in our Western world, religion has hardly any relevance anymore. The question asked in the 1970s by Christian theologian and philosopher, Francis A. Schaeffer, *How Should We Then Live?*, is answered by many with an appeal to the wisdom of philosophers, not to that of Christian leaders. Philosophers, and to some extent artists and intellectual journalists, are the spiritual leaders of the Western world, as was the case in the pre-Christian age. In some cases, philosophers are not much more than intellectual journalists, analyzing our times.

Sometimes these philosophers do have a Christian confession, such as the Scottish philosopher, Alasdair MacIntyre, and the Canadian philosopher, Charles M. Taylor. They have published great works, MacIntyre on moral and political philosophy, and on the history of philosophy and theology, Taylor on social and political philosophy, and on the history of ideas. There is a lot of practical wisdom in these works. But what is lacking is an underlying coherent and encompassing cosmology and epistemology, which is rooted in the biblical ground-motive (see below).

Today, particularly in our postmodern times, such a coherent and encompassing cosmology and epistemology may seem old-fashioned to many. People do not believe in "grand narratives" anymore (see chapter 2). But they forget that what philosophers and intellectual journalists are writing *always* presupposes a certain worldview, or even a certain implicit cosmology and epistemology, for which they usually do not account, or of which they might not even be very conscious. We read such authors, we admire their intellectual wisdom, but we tend to forget this one crucial question: *Within what framework of thought are they operating*? Do I have to discover that for myself when reading them? Why would they not account for it themselves? Or do they operate from the notion that their ideas are "neutral," "objective," and "unprejudiced"? Now, *that* would be really old-fashioned!

Faith and Beliefs

The next question is one which you yourself have probably already thought about. Is there anything that underlies our worldview? Or is our worldview the most profound basis for all our scientific theories? The answer to the second question is a clear No. Our worldview itself is founded upon our faith. You may argue: But my worldview is my faith! My reply to this is: No, your worldview is a set of *beliefs*, but your *faith* is much more than that. Your faith underlies your beliefs. Try to follow me! Your beliefs are (more or less) rational, but your faith is what I would call supra-rational, that is, it transcends (rises above) the rational. Note carefully: faith is not non-rational, or even irrational; faith is not necessarily *against* reason, but faith is certainly *above* reason. It is important to grasp this distinction. Absurdities (like a square circle) are illogical, they are *against* reason. By contrast, mysteries surpass human logic, they are *above* reason.

Again I repeat: beliefs are rational, whereas faith is supra-rational. Your beliefs are often connected with certain affections, emotions, logical and moral considerations, lingual formulations (i.e., thoughts formulated in language), social relationships, etc. But your faith is above all that: it transcends all your affections, emotions, logical and moral considerations, lingual formulations, social relationships, etc. In other words, it is not only supra-rational, but also—as I call it—supra-sensitive, supra-lingual, supra-social, etc.

You see, when you set out to think about science and theories, you end up with worldviews, beliefs, and even faith. You probably did not expect that, since many people think that science and faith have nothing to do with each other. The opposite is true: they are more closely interrelated than you might think.

If we speak of faith, then realize that it is people who have faith. What someone believes tells us something about what kind of person that "believing someone" is. You can also put it this way: thinking about beliefs and faith presupposes a certain idea about what, or who, Man is because it is Man who believes. I will come back later to this important matter of philosophical anthropology (the philosophy of Man; see chapter 6), but already now I have to make some introductory remarks.

I believe that Man is more than the sum total of all his functions: his physical and physiological functions, his mental functions, his logical, social, economic, juridical, and moral functions, etc. Man feels, thinks, wants, believes, acts—but who is the person who does all this feeling, thinking, wanting, believing, acting? I can say about myself: *I* feel, *I* think, *I* want, *I* believe, *I* act. But who is this *I*? I definitely believe that this I, or ego, or personality center, or whatever you call it, must be more than all this feeling, thinking, wanting, believing, and acting taken together. This is similar to the fact that a tree is more than the sum total of its trunk and branches, a church is more than the sum total of all its members, and a man's faith is more than the sum total of all his beliefs.

That is why I have said that my faith is *beyond* my beliefs; and therefore, if my beliefs are emotional, rational, lingual, social, etc., and if Man's ego is beyond all its functions, then we can draw the following conclusion: my faith is a matter of my ego, of my deepest self, beyond which there is nothing. My faith *precedes*, or *transcends*, all my beliefs, and all the emotional, rational, lingual, social (etc.) aspects of it. I can certainly *account* rationally for my beliefs, I can adduce logical arguments why I hold them, and I can give logical counterarguments when my beliefs are attacked. All aspects of that process belong to the domain of the logical, the rational. However, my deepest reasons why I prefer these arguments to those of my opponents are because I am logically-rationally convinced that my arguments are better than theirs. No, I prefer them because deep down in my heart I have supra-rational—please remember: not necessarily irrational!—reasons why I prefer them.

That deepest inner conviction, which surpasses reason, is what we call faith. This faith can be formulated in rational thoughts and words; then it becomes "beliefs." In other words, it can be logically accounted for. But this faith as such is beyond all formulating and accounting. It is always *more* than that, just as my ego is more than all my functions together. This will all be explained more extensively later; I cannot tell you everything at once!

Religion

Now we are ready to take our next step. I assert that, in the profoundest sense, faith always possesses a religious nature. Of course, that depends on my definition of "religion." The science of religion (German: *Religionswissenschaft*; Dutch: *godsdienstwetenschap*) supplies us with many definitions of religion. Such definitions have nothing to do with Christianity, Judaism, Islam, Buddhism, Hinduism, etc. as such, but with the characteristics that all such world religions have in common—the characteristics that make religion to be religion. The most important factor that all such religions have in common seems to be that religion is the confidence Man has in Someone or something as a kind of Ultimate Ground. This Ultimate Ground may be God, or some god, or many gods, or more vaguely, something divine, Someone or something that surpasses all visible things, or something *within* the visible world. This Someone or something functions as a kind of general, foundational principle from which the whole of reality can be explained. Such a principle could be number, matter, life, the spiritual, reason, development (evolution), society—or even sex, football, fashion, alcohol, etc.

For the time being, let us say that it does not matter in what you believe. My point is rather that you *do* believe in Someone or something, some ultimate reality, or ultimate part or principle of reality. For you, this Someone or something, this element or principle, explains the whole of reality, gives reality its meaning and purpose (or denies it any meaning or purpose), and is the thing in which you place your ultimate confidence, or to which you are ultimately committed. It is some Ultimate Ground to which your feeling, thinking, willing, and believing resorts, and beyond which these have nothing else to resort to.

Even if you are an atheist, there is some Ultimate Ground for all your thinking, namely, the supra-rational conviction that there is no god. Even if you are an agnostic, there is some Ultimate Ground for all your thinking, namely, the supra-rational conviction that people cannot know if there is a god. Even if you are a nihilist—you believe that there is no meaning or purpose in reality, or even that nothing exists—then nihilism is the Ultimate Ground for all your feeling, thinking, wanting, and believing. Even if you are a solipsist—you believe you cannot prove there is anything outside yourself—then your solipsism is your Ultimate Ground of certainty, of your deep inner conviction.

Even if you think that it is impossible to have certain deep inner convictions, then this is your deep inner conviction. If you are an absolute relativist, then this relativism is your Absolute, in which you have full confidence. (The most clever relativists are those who relativize even their own relativism, but even then, their relativism is their Ultimate Ground.)

Atheism, agnosticism, nihilism, solipsism are "-isms" that can be logically explained, that can be formulated in words, and that can be rationally accounted for. Even irrationalism is a viewpoint that can be, and is, rationally accounted for. But in the end these "-isms" cannot be rationally demonstrated beyond any doubt any more than faith in God can, for that matter. That is the very reason why we call such convictions *faith*. Faith is beyond the rational (and beyond the emotional, the lingual, the social, etc.), and yet it is certainty: a supra-rational, existential certainty of the heart. It is our "ultimate commitment."

This supra-rational, existential ultimate confidence or commitment I call *religious*, for this is exactly what religion in the broadest sense is all about: a supra-rational, existential confidence in some Ultimate Ground. Even if you are a staunch rationalist, your faith in rationalism cannot itself be rational—it precedes reason. You cannot rationally prove that it is more rational to be rational than to be irrational, because that would be a circular argument. Your faith in rationalism is not necessarily irrational, but it is certainly supra-rational, it precedes and surpasses reason, and as such has an existential, ultimate character, which by definition I call religious.

This, to my mind, is an interesting conclusion of my reasoning. Your scientific knowledge is ultimately rooted in your philosophical convictions, these convictions are ultimately rooted in your worldview, and your worldview is ultimately rooted in your supra-rational, existential faith, which by definition is of a religious nature. That may be quite surprising to you! There is no scientific knowledge without ultimately some kind of religion, even if it is atheism, agnosticism, nihilism, solipsism, rationalism, materialism—or Christianity, for that matter.

Christian Philosophy

This leads us to the second question I asked at the beginning of this chapter. What is Christian philosophy? In order to answer this question, it might seem at first glance that we have to resort to the defensive. For it is clear that most philosophers in this world, and even in the Western world, are not Christians at all. Many philosophers are not even religious in the usual sense of the word: they are not Christians, not practicing Jews, not Muslims, etc. Some philosophers in the Western world *are* Christians, but they often keep their philosophical work and their Christian beliefs quite separate. They may belong, or have belonged, to one of the most popular philosophical schools—determinism, utilitarianism, (neo)positivism, objectivism, existentialism, analytical philosophy, postmodernism, some liberation philosophy, some feminist philosophy, you name it—without their Christian convictions being fundamentally involved.

To put it a bit bluntly: on Sundays and in their free time, they are Christians, and during working hours they work within some neutral, secular philosophical framework. They are Christians-and-philosophers, but not Christian philosophers. That is, they do not adhere to, or even reject outrightly, the notion of a Christian philosophy, often because of some idea of a neutral, objective, unbiased, or unprejudiced philosophy. I have tried to show that such a philosophy is impossible, and I will give some more evidence in subsequent chapters.

Now if it is true that philosophy is always rooted in some faith, and that this faith is ultimately of some religious nature, then all philosophy is, at its deepest level, religious in nature. I cannot see how I could possibly avoid that conclusion. Just as *all* thinking, and *all* feeling, *all* wanting, *all* believing, at its deepest level, is religious in nature, for that matter. If this is right, then the choice is not between common, current (that is, secular) philosophy and some religiously biased philosophy, but *between philosophy based on false religion, and philosophy based on true religion*. If the former choice were correct, I would not hesitate to choose the first option I mentioned. But if indeed all philosophy is ultimately religious in nature, then I would certainly prefer a philosophy based on true religion.

Now you may have begun to understand why I think we can truly speak of a Christian philosophy. I am a Christian, so for me, true philosophy cannot be anything else than a Christian philosophy. There is no such thing as a neutral philosophy, so I prefer a Christian philosophy. I truly believe that such a philosophy is not only possible, but it is also highly desirable, even necessary. Many young Christians go to college or university nowadays. They study some scientific discipline, but unfortunately very often without realizing the basic questions of such sciences. In many cases, nobody teaches them about these questions. Even less does anyone help these students to realize how their Christian beliefs are involved in answering these preliminary philosophical questions. In other words, they do not know how to address the problems with which they are confronted, in an appropriate Christian-philosophical way. They may be indoctrinated with the idea of a neutral, objective philosophy, and even lose their faith in that pursuit. This has happened many times. That is why I wrote this book.

True and False Religion

In the end, as I said, there are only two kinds of scientific enterprise: the one based on true religion, and the one based on false religion. But in practice, the matter is much more complicated, of course. On the one hand, any science based on true religion may still be full of mistakes and human errors. A good starting-point does not guarantee good results. Christians may do science in a way that is not very scholarly. Though you may begin with a perfect faith, you may nevertheless end up with poor science.

On the other hand, even science that is ultimately based on some false religion can certainly come up with partial truth elements, or to put it more carefully, with certain valid statements about reality. They may be valid, firstly, because they have not been refuted so far; secondly, because they seem reasonable within the framework of what we already know, or seem to know; and thirdly, because they "work," that is, using them leads to good practical results. For practical people—and many Christians, too, are very practical people—this is all that matters. They follow a pragmatic approach: it does not matter whether a theory is true— whatever that may mean—but only whether it works. These are also people who in general are not very interested in philosophy. They are not the people for whom this book has been written (although, keep on reading; you *might* get interested after all!).

This book is for those who *are* interested in the basic questions behind the various sciences, including the (complicated) matter of truth (see especially chapter 10). Being interested in such questions means being interested in philosophy. And if you are a Christian, you may be pleased to find out that there is a Christian way of doing philosophy—a way that is rooted in the Christian faith. You do not have to be ashamed of being interested in Christian philosophy, for the alternatives are Jewish, Islamic, Buddhist,

Hindu, materialist, rationalist, socialist, liberal, nihilist, positivist philosophies (and so many more). Ultimately, they are *all* of a religious nature. So why not choose a philosophy that is of one piece with your own Christian beliefs?

Please note, a Christian philosophy does not mean a biblical philosophy, if by this term you mean that we could get such a Christian philosophy directly out of the Bible. Scripture does not teach philosophy, or any other science; the Bible does not presuppose any philosophy, nor does it supply us with indirect philosophical statements. Only if you have some very vague idea about philosophy—as if it were the same thing as doctrine or teaching—you might come up with the idea that the Bible addresses philosophical problems as such. It does not. Philosophy is very theoretical, and the Bible never is.

However, through our Christian beliefs, Scripture certainly supplies us with the building blocks for a Christian *worldview,* or view of life! Within Christian philosophy, the Bible operates in an indirect way. Scripture does not speak the abstract, theoretical language of science, including philosophy, but the practical language of our everyday life. It is interested in our daily matters, it speaks the language of faith. As such, it does not address the typical theoretical problems of science. But indirectly, through our Christian worldview, it definitely does affect the sciences, including philosophy.

Questions for Review

1. What three important questions needed to be answered in this chapter?

2. Why does studying something in a scientific way require answering philosophical questions?

3. What are the two "legs" on which philosophy stands?

4. According to this chapter, what is philosophy?

5. What comes first—philosophy or worldview—and why?

6. What is the difference between your worldview and your faith? Between your faith and your beliefs?

7. Is faith rational? Why (or why not)?

8. In what sense can we claim that every person is religious?

9. Defend the legitimacy of "Christian philosophy."

10. Why is a Christian philosophy not the same thing as a biblical philosophy?

Chapter Two

KNOWLEDGE AND WISDOM

Philosophy and Science

The term "philosophy" comes from the Greek word *philosophia* and means "love for wisdom." Philosophy has the goal of offering us some kind of wisdom. The term "science" comes from the Latin word *scientia* and means "knowledge," in this case scientific, that is, theoretical knowledge. The terms "theoretical" and "theory" come from the Greek word *theoria*, which is derived from a word for "seeing, looking, beholding, contemplating." It is related to our word *theatre*, which is a place where people "look" at something happening on the stage. How are such basic notions as wisdom, knowledge, and seeing interrelated?

The term "wisdom," just like the old-fashioned English verb "to wit," and just like the German and Dutch words *wissen* and *weten* ("to know, to wit"), and *Wissenschaft* and *wetenschap* ("science") respectively, come from an Indo-European radical *wid-*, which means "to see." Latin, Greek, French, German, Dutch, English, and many other languages belong to the family of Indo-European languages. Think of the Latin word *video*, which means "I see." The Greek word *oida* (originally *woida*) means "I know," but literally it is a perfect tense of *(w)eidon* (related in turn to the verb *horaō*), which means "I have seen."

If "witting" comes from "seeing," does this mean that, even today, true knowledge is based on seeing? Many people would argue that knowledge is based rather on thinking. In the history of human thought this has often been a central question: What is the origin of true wisdom—seeing or thinking? Philosophers, that is, lovers of wisdom, should certainly be interested in this question.

Our Western mind-set is rooted in two quite different approaches to this problem. One was the Jewish-Christian approach. It was in accord with the foundational meaning of "wisdom" and "witting," and answered: True science, or true wisdom, or true

17

philosophy, stems from what you have *seen*; in the ultimate sense this means what God has revealed to you. This is why we call a certain piece of wisdom a *view* or an *insight*, two words that come from viewing and seeing. (Think of what we said in the previous chapter about our world*view* and our *"view* of life.")

The other root of our Western mind-set was the approach of classical antiquity. This was rather a way of thinking: true science, or wisdom, or philosophy is based upon (logical, rational, intellectual) *thought*. The gods may deceive you, or there might be no gods at all. Your eyes and ears may also deceive you; you may fall into the snare of optical illusions. In the end, you can trust only in what you yourself have logically thought out and thought through. If you obey the rules of logic, rational thinking will lead you to sure knowledge, something the "seers," as well as your sense organs, can never supply you with.

It is striking that the ancient wisdom books of the Hindus are called *Veda*, a word that means "I know," but a word that stems from the same Indo-European root "I see." The wisdom offered in these books is based on seeing rather than on thinking. In all ancient cultures the truly wise person was the person who had "seen," that is, seen in the divine world. That person received predictive dreams, or heard inward voices, received visions (another word derived from *videre*, "to see"), and "saw" the answers to the big questions in ominous signs and other symbols. In Germanic paganism it was the same. One of the old English words for a magician is *wizard*, which literally means "wise man," and the word *witch* comes from the Saxon word *wicca*, "wise." Wizards and witches were considered to be the wise people, the people who "knew," and they knew because they had "seen" things in the invisible world.

In fact, in ancient Israel it was the same: the spiritual leaders of the people were the prophets. The main characteristic of the prophet was that he had "seen"; therefore, the prophet was originally called a "seer" (e.g., 1 Sam. 9:9). Of course, this cannot be severed from "hearing" (cf. Rom. 10:14, 17); in the Jewish-Christian tradition, the "Word" plays a central role. But the pivotal point is this: true wisdom is not primarily that which you have worked out in your own thinking, but that which you have seen or heard from the divine world. Seeing and hearing do not go very well without thinking, but if you assume you can think without having "seen," then you are an impoverished person, the ancients might have said.

In ancient Greece, at the outset of Greek thinking, it was not any different. Ancient poets like Homer and Hesiod found the explanation for the reality they described in the world of the gods. Even the earliest Greek philosophers—"lovers of wisdom," remember?—were rather "seers" than "thinkers." Parmenides (fifth century B.C.) was the first who explicitly placed theoretical knowledge on the foundation of thinking—but he wrote down his ideas in a poem that began with announcing that what was to follow had been revealed to him in a vision. His contemporary Heraclitus, too, was in fact at least as much a seer as a thinker. It was only in the time of Plato and Aristotle (fourth century B.C.) that the wise man, i.e. the philosopher, became a man of pure reason, a thinker. Wisdom is no longer found *outside* Man, in that which people behold and hear in higher realms, but *within* Man, in pure intellect. And even then, in Plato's thinking the visionary had not entirely died out.

To Plato and Aristotle and their successors, we owe that remarkable phenomenon that we call *philosophy*, from which at later stages the various special sciences were derived. In the later Greek and Roman period, the first special sciences came into being: mathematics (Euclid), medicine (Hippocrates and Galen), and physics (Archimedes). Aristotle could be called one of the first natural scientists. Other special sciences came much later. Even in the eighteenth century, biology was still largely a philosophical discipline, particularly subservient to natural theology (i.e., the search in nature for signs that could demonstrate the existence of God). Psychology was, even until about 1875, nothing but a branch of philosophy, and only afterwards developed into an experimental (experience oriented) science.

Two Roots

In the ancient Greek world, Western philosophy began at the moment it severed itself from the visionary approach, from religion and mythology. As a consequence, it began asking specific questions that even today are challenges to the minds of philosophers and special scientists. As long as Man was still a captive of mythical thinking, he did not even think of asking questions like those. And if he had thought of them, he would have answered them from what he had "seen" and "heard" in the world of the gods. As long as people handle such basic questions in such an uncritical way, no science can develop in the present-day sense of the term. For instance, as long as people consider nature to be as fickle and capricious as their own gods, they will not search for basic regularities in nature that we call natural laws. But this is the very thing the natural sciences are all about.

In order to arrive at science as we understand it, one does not have to give up one's belief in the gods, or God. Otherwise, no philosophy or science on a Christian basis would be possible in the first place. On the contrary, it was *because* of their belief in the God of the Bible that the great sixteenth- and seventeenth-century pioneers of the modern natural sciences (Nicolaus Copernicus, Johannes Kepler, Galileo Galilei, Isaac Newton, Robert Boyle;) learned to believe in a fixed law-order, or world order. This is the belief that everything in the cosmos is subject to fixed laws, and not to the whims of gods and spirits. They knew about the world-order and about these fixed laws because they knew the *Lawgiver*, the God of the Bible.

The second necessary thing was that, on the basis of this law-order, people tried to find causes for every cosmic phenomenon within that same cosmic reality. In philosophy and science, one is never allowed to appeal to the world of gods and spirits, or to God, in order to explain mysterious phenomena. The great pioneers of the modern natural sciences were convinced of this, not because they rejected God–on the contrary, they believed in him–but because they were convinced that God had created the cosmos in such a way that the cosmos itself would come up with the answers about what regularities God had placed within it.

Here we have a clear example of the double origin of our Western philosophy. It was not in Israel, but in ancient Greece that the first philosophers rose to prominence, thinkers who began to approach certain basic questions about cosmic reality in a purely rational way, and no longer with an uncritical appeal to some mythical world. But at the same time the danger arose that

that other ancient approach, i.e., knowing by "seeing"—Christians would say, knowing through divine revelation—would get lost. Therefore, it was extremely important for Western culture that it would not only borrow from the "thinking" inheritance of the ancient Greeks but also from the "seeing" inheritance of the Jewish-Christian culture. Without the latter's biblical wisdom, it is highly unlikely that in the sixteenth and seventeenth centuries the foundation could have been laid for modern natural sciences in the way I have just explained.

Very often, the two ways, the way of seeing and the way of thinking, were in danger of drifting apart. Time and again, people arose who wanted to save biblical wisdom from the claws of worldly science and fell back upon the way of seeing only. Or people arose who wanted to save science from the claws of rigid biblical tradition by resorting to the way of thinking only. It is my conviction that the two ways must stay together, and that this will be a blessing for our civilization. In my opinion, this means that science should remain embedded in biblical wisdom in terms of the manner in which it has achieved theoretical expression in Christian philosophy.

Early Christianity and the Middle Ages

The Greek philosophers preferred thinking to seeing. This was, of course, a matter of faith. If you think that it is more logical to base your wisdom on thinking than on seeing, you land in a circular argument: you *start* with logic in order to show that it is better to be logical than to be non-logical (like starting from seeing). Therefore I say that the Greek replaced their old faith—based on seeing—by a new faith: the preference for thinking. This is faith in reason, and this faith has dominated Western thinking for more than two thousand three hundred years, until the twentieth century.

The church fathers clearly saw the enormous danger of Greek philosophy for early Christianity. The Greeks considered their philosophy to be "true theology" because within their philosophy they spoke in a "scientific" way about God. For the church fathers this was unacceptable. The great Augustine (354-430) turned the matter upside down: according to him, (Christian) theology was the "true philosophy." He even claimed that the true Christian was the true philosopher.

In fact, to this very day many Christians still hold Augustine's position. They argue that we do not need any Christian philosophy because we already have theology. They forget that theology attempts to answer only *theological* questions. It has no answers to, and does not even deal with, typically *philosophical* questions, such as: What is knowledge? What is science? What is nature? What is culture? It does have *theological* things to say about these and many other matters, but the things theology says are not of a fundamental significance for all sciences. Theology does not have, and never had, the task of functioning as a foundational science for all the special sciences, from mathematics to the humanities. In fact, theology itself is nothing but one of the many special sciences, which has its own basic philosophical questions, such as: What is theology? Is it science, and if so, what kind of science? How does it relate to the other special sciences? As a theoretical enterprise, how does it relate to practical faith knowledge? What are its specific scientific methods?

In my humble opinion, both the Greeks and Augustine were mistaken: philosophy is not the true theology, and theology is not the true philosophy. Unlike the Greeks, Augustine did see, though, that human reason is *not* autonomous. That is, reason cannot find the truth without the enlightenment of divine revelation. This was a fundamental insight, still valid in Christian philosophy. Augustine wrote: *Crede ut intelligas,* "Believe, so that you may understand." Faith precedes, and underlies, and preconditions, reason. (Precisely how this happens is a matter we will investigate more closely later in this book.)

In the thirteenth century, Thomas Aquinas proposed a very different solution: philosophy is not the true theology, and theology is not the true philosophy, no, the two have to be clearly distinguished. However, for this very reason, he was strongly opposed to the notion of a *Christian* philosophy, that is, a philosophy based on a Christian worldview, inspired by Scripture. On the contrary, he claimed that philosophy is an autonomous science. This means that philosophy is a science independent of any foundation outside itself, based exclusively upon human reason *severed from faith*. He considered Christian theology to be some supernatural, even sacred science, highly elevated above natural philosophy and all special sciences. Supernatural theology is done by the light of divine revelation—and is therefore sacred—whereas natural philosophy, as well as all the special sciences, are done by the light of autonomous reason. Again, this view is still quite dominant among theologians. (Thomas's philosophy, *Thomism*, is the official philosophy of the Roman Catholic Church.)

It should be emphasized that Thomas Aquinas at least tried to keep theology and philosophy together. But a later thinker, William of Occam (1285-1349), considered this to be hopeless. He severed theology entirely from philosophy, rejected the notion of natural theology with its so-called proofs for the existence of God, and kept divine revelation and human reason entirely separate. With him and his successors, faith and reason got divorced forever. From then on, faith and science, faith and philosophy, had nothing to do with each other. William of Occam even used a slogan that, in a somewhat different form, had been used by the church father Tertullian: *credo quia absurdum*, "I believe because it is absurd." That is, my beliefs are fully outside the domain of reason. In my terminology, Occam considered faith to be non-rational, or even irrational, instead of supra-rational.

So far, we have found four solutions to the puzzle of the relationship between faith and reason: (1) reason superseding faith; (2) faith superseding reason; (3) distinguishing faith and reason but keeping them together; and (4) separating faith and reason altogether. The question now arises: Is there a fifth solution?

The Modern Age

The Reformation (sixteenth century) completely rejected the separation introduced by William of Occam. Perhaps one of the greatest rediscoveries of the Reformers was the notion that God's Word has authority over *all* domains of cosmic reality, including philosophy and the special sciences, and all human thought. They did away with the separation between faith and science. What a great idea: a Reformational philosophy founded upon the Word of God! Alas, nothing really changed in practice. No Christian starting points for the various special sciences were developed. I do not blame the Reformers; probably, it was simply too early for that. The Reformers, Martin Luther and John Calvin, preached a clear gospel about God's Word having sway over all of human life. They pushed medieval philosophy out through the front door. But their successors, Philipp Melanchthon and Theodore Beza, reintroduced medieval philosophy through the back door. Again, do not blame them too severely: they simply did so because they had nothing better to work with.

Interestingly, it was not a Reformational but a Roman Catholic thinker, Blaise Pascal (1623-1662), who claimed that the "God of the philosophers," for whom the philosophers kindly reserved some room in their thinking, had little to do with the God of the Bible. In his famous *Pensées* ("Thoughts"), he stated, with a beautiful word play, that the *heart* has its own reasons (for believing), of which *reason* knows nothing. Faith does not have to fight for its little place under the sun. On the contrary, it underlies and preconditions all human thinking (see the previous chapter).

In spite of the efforts of the Reformers and of Pascal, the separation between faith and reason, between faith and philosophy, was maintained. Reason, along with rationalism, dominated Christian thinking. This rationalism was so strong that, as the Enlightenment, (seventeenth and eighteenth centuries) began, Christian thinking had no real defense against it. "Dare to use your own intellect," was the slogan of the great German philosopher, Immanuel Kant (1724-1804), with which he described what he saw as the essence of the Enlightenment. This did not mean that Kant removed God from his thinking. Rather, his noble motive was to save Christian faith from the claws of the natural sciences. He did so by assigning faith its own safe corner. But, according to him, the whole of natural life belonged to the domain of pure reason. Many of the Enlightenment thinkers allowed God and religion their own little place—but only within the domain of religious life, the life of prayer, praise, and preaching. From the domain of philosophy, from the special sciences, and from societal life, religion was banned forever. That is what we call secularization.

The Twentieth Century

Actually, this is a tragedy. During all these centuries, Christian thinking had been very much occupied with theological questions, which moreover had often been dealt with in a very rationalistic way. No one had succeeded in defining in a satisfactory way the relationship between faith and reason, and between faith and philosophy. Hardly anyone seemed even interested. As I have said before, perhaps the time for this was simply not yet ripe.

After the enormous optimism of the nineteenth century, also in philosophy, the twentieth century began with its tremendous disillusionments. These were exemplified in the First World War and the Russian Revolution, but also in great scientific crises; think especially of Albert Einstein in physics, and Sigmund Freud in psychology, to say nothing of Neo-Darwinism. The theories of Freud broke away from the idea that intellectual people are led entirely by reason. They may *think* they are led by their *thinking*, but in reality they are led as much by feelings, memories, prejudices, unconscious drives and instincts over which they have no control. The notion that Man is above all else a *rational* being has collapsed.

For the first time, after so many centuries of optimistic rationalism, philosophy became a problem to itself; or rather, Western Man became a problem to himself. He did not know anymore who he was, and he no longer knew what science was all about. Therefore, it was no wonder that both philosophical anthropology and the philosophy of science came to the forefront. As long as Man and science were taken for granted, there was no need to develop a philosophical anthropology or a philosophy of science.

I have often felt that these two branches of philosophy coming to full blossom was a prerequisite to the development of a truly Christian philosophy. Consider, for a moment, the philosophy of science: how tremendously important is the insight of many pioneers (Michael Polanyi, Karl Popper, Imre Lakatos, Thomas Kuhn) that science does not start with observations or logical arguments, but with *beliefs*. And these beliefs do not belong primarily to the domain of reason but to deeper layers of our conscious, subconscious, and unconscious.

For the first time in Western history, it began to dawn on people that reason is *not* necessarily the alpha and omega (the starting point and goal) of philosophy and science. Of course, reason is not discarded by science. Not at all. Even if you are an irrationalist, you need reason to argue your position. However, irrationalism and supra-rationalism—which are not the same, as we have already seen—have finally assigned to reason its own proper place. An important place, to be sure, but reason is not everything. Many other factors, affections, emotions, memories, prejudices, preconceived ideas, social and economic and moral notions, and yes, "even" religious beliefs, often play an essential role in all human enterprise, including philosophy and science.

Reformational Philosophy

The insights I have just mentioned paved the way for a Christian philosophy that based all thinking, practical and theoretical, upon (supra-rational) faith. The greatest Christian thinker who developed this notion was the Dutch philosopher, Herman Dooyeweerd (1894-1977), professor of the philosophy of law at the Free University of Amsterdam. Many other Christian philosophers began to think along the same lines. I cannot mention them all; I limit myself to those I think were the most influential: his brother-in-law, Dirk H.Th. Vollenhoven (1892-1978) in the Netherlands, professor of philosophy at the Free University, and Hendrik G. Stoker (1899-1993) in South Africa, at the Potchefstroom University. Among the second generation, we find philosophers such as Hendrik van Riessen (1911-2000) and Andree Troost (1916-2009) in the Netherlands, to name only a few from whom I have learned so much, and H. Evan Runner (1916-2002) in the United States.

To illustrate the significance of Dooyeweerd, let me quote not some followers, but some outsiders. On the occasion of Dooyeweerd's seventieth birthday, G.E. Langemeijer, attorney general of the Dutch Appeal Court and chairman of the Royal Dutch Academy of Sciences, wrote that Dooyeweerd was "the most original philosopher the Netherlands has ever produced, even Spinoza not excepted." Paul B. Cliteur, a well-known Dutch atheist and president of the Humanist League in the Netherlands, wrote in 1994: "Herman Dooyeweerd is undoubtedly the most formidable Dutch philosopher of the 20th century. . . . As a humanist I have always looked at 'my own tradition' in search of similar examples. They simply don't exist. Of course, humanists too wrote important books, but in the case of Herman Dooyeweerd we are justified in speaking about a philosopher of international repute." Giorgio del Vecchio, an Italian neo-Kantian philosopher, viewed Dooyeweerd as "the most profound, innovative, and penetrating philosopher since Kant." And American philosopher Alvin Plantinga stated that "Dooyeweerd's work was comprehensive, insightful, profound, courageous, and quite properly influential."

Religious Ground-Motives (1)

In answering the question about what governs the thinking of philosophers, Dooyeweerd introduced his notion *of religious ground-motives*. These are the deepest motives—therefore he called them *ground*-motives—that drive our hearts, and are therefore, almost by definition (see our previous chapter), of a religious nature. They go even deeper than the so-called "unconscious" of Freud and other psychologists. Operating from the heart, these ground-motives govern our feelings, our will, our rational deliberations, our social and moral decisions, etc. Like many other philosophers of science in the twentieth century, Dooyeweerd concluded that science is not neutral, and not objective, that is, not purely rooted in reason alone. And even if philosophy were thoroughly rational, this rationality would be governed by a religious ground-motive.

In this manner, Dooyeweerd broke away from the idea of autonomous reason and of an unprejudiced science, and thus from the false separation between faith and science that had plagued Western thinking for so many centuries. Like all thinking, philosophical and scientific thinking originates from the human *heart*, and thus from *faith*. Man finds the ultimate ground for all his thinking and all his existence in the God of the Bible—or in some other god, some ultimate principle, some ideology, some "-ism," that functions for him as the Ultimate Ground of his deepest convictions, of his ultimate commitment.

The insight that science always rests in faith of some kind became widespread in the twentieth century. Influential non-Christian philosophers like Karl R. Popper showed that science never starts with objectively collecting facts, but always with a hypothesis, which is a *belief*. Imre Lakatos showed that people do not easily give up their hypotheses, their theories, but do everything within their power to safeguard their beliefs. And Thomas S. Kuhn pointed to the many non-rational factors that determine the course of science, including even religious factors.

Modern Philosophical Schools

The profound twentieth-century conviction that reason is not everything led to all kinds of philosophical schools with which Christian philosophy has actually very little in common. But at least they have helped us to see how the supremacy of reason came to its end, and thereby created room for a Christian approach to philosophy. First, there was existentialism, a school in which human existence is the focus of attention. Existentialists, such as the German philosopher Martin Heidegger (1889-1976) and the French philosopher Jean-Paul Sartre (1905-1980), wrote about the absurdity of human existence, the absolute insufficiency of reason, and an irrational way out, an escape from the modern impasse. Nineteenth-century rationalistic cultural *optimism* had given way to twentieth-century irrationalistic cultural *pessimism*.

Another current is (or by now, was?) the New Age movement, inspired by Eastern philosophy. That is the belief in a new astrological age, starting somewhere in the second half of the twentieth century. In this New Age, the emphasis would lie much less on analytical reason, which breaks everything apart into small pieces, but rather on synthetic (or as New Agers like to say, holistic) thinking. This is thinking in large totalities, a thinking springing from feeling, intuition, and even paranormal (psychic) capacities. New Age thinkers claim that the results of modern physics, with its unpredictabilities, surprisingly correspond with the ideas of ancient Eastern mysticism (Fritjof Capra, b. 1939). Again, faith and reason come very close together here.

A third current I want to mention is postmodernism. Again, this is a typical product of twentieth-century pessimism. People are tired of all the grand ideals of the Enlightenment, such as the universal validity of reason, of reason allegedly solving all our problems, of the power of science and technology allegedly rendering life more elevated and pleasant. Today we realize that humanity has more problems than ever, as an actual consequence of science and technology. What did science produce? Wonderful machines that have taken over a lot of our work—as well as producing larger unemployment. Wonderful medicines that ease and extend our lives—as well as producing overpopulation and new diseases, to say nothing of abortion and euthanasia. A wonderful increase of agricultural harvests—as well as greater poverty and hunger in the world, and a frightening exploitation of nature. Wonderful industrial products—as well as devastating nuclear weapons, chemical and biological weapons, genetic manipulation, horrible environmental pollution, and heinous mountains of waste.

Some postmodernists (like Jean-François Lyotard, 1924-1998) claim that the time of the "grand narratives" (or meta-narratives) is over. Among these grand narratives, they reckon all traditional religions, but also all philosophical and political thought-systems, worldviews, and ideologies, and even the quantum-mechanical worldview and evolutionism. In particular, the Enlightenment faith in reason has been *unmasked*. Postmodernists have not stopped thinking rationally, but human reason has lost its universal validity. Truth—whatever that may be, who can tell?—consists at best of small pieces, which can be different for everyone and can contradict each other without difficulty.

Faith, Reason, Feeling

How could a Christian escape the present impasse? That is a big question. At any rate, we know how we *cannot* make such an escape. It does not help a bit to replace the power of reason with the power of feeling and intuition. Throughout history, people have tried that, and they have failed. In the twentieth century, existentialism and New Age tried the same thing, and failed. Over against the supremacy of reason, I place *faith*. Don't make the mistake of identifying faith with feeling! Faith is beyond feeling, just as faith is beyond reason, because it has to do with the existential condition of our transcendent *heart*. Faith can, and does, *express* itself in (sensitive) feelings, (rational) deliberations, (social, moral, etc.) decisions, but at the same time faith is always beyond them.

Faith is *transcendent*; it surpasses everything that belongs to our empirical world, that is, the world of our human observations. Feelings, deliberations, and decisions, however, are *immanent*: they are part of our empirical world. Remember these two terms; they can be very helpful. Faith is *transcendent*, reason and feeling are *immanent*. Man's heart—his ego, his personality center—is transcendent, Man's (sensitive) feelings, (rational) deliberations, and (social, moral, etc.) decisions are immanent. Feelings, deliberations, and decisions are immanent functions of the transcendent heart; the heart expresses itself through them. The functions are, as Dooyeweerd has put it, the immanent ramifications of the transcendent heart, and the heart is, so to speak, the transcendent focal point or concentration point of all its functions.

Read these sentences again! We will come back to this matter, but already now, it is very helpful to grasp the distinction between the transcendent and immanent, between the heart and its functions. It will help you never to confuse the heart with feeling, or to confuse our transcendent faith with our immanent beliefs or emotions. Faith can always be *expressed* in beliefs and emotions, but at the same time faith always *transcends* our beliefs and emotions. If I love my wife, I can express this in words and actions, but my love as such is always much more than all my sweet words and actions taken together.

Several times now, I have used the term *heart*. Of course, I do not mean by this the muscle that pumps blood in our chest. The term *heart*, as a metaphor for our innermost being, our ego, our personality center, is very well known in our everyday language, and also in the Bible. Proverbs 4:23 says, "Above all else, guard your heart, for everything you do flows from it" (TNIV). I know it is always dangerous to read philosophical language into the Bible—I definitely do not want to do that—but let me suggest that this proverb is describing with the phrase "everything you do" what I have called the functions of the heart. This proverb seems to say that all my feelings, my deliberations, and my decisions flow from the heart; feeling, thinking, desiring, and believing are functions of the heart. *Believing* is one of my immanent functions, just like feeling and thinking; but *faith* is the condition of my transcendent heart, from which all my immanent functions such as feeling, thinking, and believing flow forth.

If you learn to make this kind of distinction, you will easily see that something like autonomous reason cannot exist at all. In other words, a separation between faith and reason is impossible. If you had to answer the question what is the main difference between animals and Man, chances are high that your answer would be quite traditional. It might run like this: "Humans are gifted with reason; animals are not." So you think reason is the most typical feature of Man? Then you really are a typical product of the Greek-Western philosophical worldview. In the Bible, the *heart* is the most typical feature of Man. I believe it would be better to say, "Humans are gifted with the capacity of *faith*—though this often deteriorates into unbelief—but animals are not." Man *is* a rational being—but he is also a sensitive, a historical, a lingual, a social, and an economic being. None of these immanent functions, however, expresses what, or who, he really is. Man is, above all, a *religious* being.

Reason is never autonomous because it is always directed by the heart. And the heart is the seat of faith. The heart is directed by faith (in the biblical sense), or by unbelief, or by a mixture of both. Therefore, no neutral, objective science can exist, simply because no neutral, objective people can exist. In the same way, there cannot be any separation between faith and science, because a science without starting-points of faith is inconceivable. You can have faith without science, but you cannot possibly have science without faith.

In the Bible, faith is always something that preconditions, and involves, rational deliberations but at the same time surpasses them. Your academic knowledge consists of a large number of facts and formulations, and hopefully some insight into the coherence between these facts. That academic knowledge hardly ever rises above the purely rational. The situation is not that much different with the knowledge of the average scientist. Usually, he (or she) is not very concerned with so-called "starting-points of faith" in his particular scientific discipline. Often he is not very conscious of how strongly his presuppositions affect the results of his scientific work. The most frequent cause of this is a high degree of specialization, so that the scientist does not see the broad scope of his science anymore, and hardly notices its pre-scientific suppositions and conditions.

Some Special Points

Let me emphasize here a point that I have mentioned before. Faith-knowledge surpasses the rational, but that does not mean it is *ir*rational. Going *beyond* reason is not the same as going *against* reason (although many people would like to say they are the same). Once I heard a man say, "I believe the whale swallowed Jonah, and if the Bible had said Jonah swallowed the whale, I would have believed that, too." I do not think that God is very pleased with that kind of faith. Gullible people, who are prepared to swallow anything, actually do not have a real faith. Biblical faith does not imply we believe all kinds of nonsense. In that respect, believers certainly do not subscribe to the slogan I mentioned before: *credo quia absurdum*, "I believe because it is absurd."

Another important point to be underscored is that biblical faith is not a package of logical—or not so logical—beliefs, but primarily a relationship of confidence. Jesus says that eternal life means knowing God (John 17:3), not in the sense of having (theological) knowledge *about* God but having intimacy *with* God (cf. 1 John 1:1-4). Knowledge in the biblical sense is much more than the intellectual knowledge with which we are so familiar in our Western culture. In the Bible, knowledge is not primarily *information* but *relation*. Adam "knew" his wife, as the old King James Version states; this means that Adam was intimate with her (Gen. 4:1; cf. Matt. 1:25). Knowledge in the biblical sense is intimacy. It is fellowship with someone, with God in particular.

In a similar way, faith is not simply accepting something to be true. I am sure Abraham Lincoln lived, but I do not have a relationship with him. Faith is trusting God, or more strongly, *entrusting yourself* to God. That is not something that leaves reason aside; it is not a blind leap in the dark. On the contrary, faith has a clear rational aspect. A believer can adduce arguments as to why it is more clever to believe in the God of the Bible than not to believe in him. We even have a whole science, called apologetics, whose task it is to supply us with rational arguments defending the Christian faith. At the same time, you realize as a believer that entrusting yourself to God is far more than all apologetic arguments together.

No rational argument as such can renew your heart; that is a miracle of the Holy Spirit (John 3:3-5; Titus 3:5). Preaching the gospel may *convince* people rationally, but only the Holy Spirit *convicts* people in their hearts. Everyone who possesses this divine persuasion of the heart feels differently, thinks differently, wills differently, believes differently, hopes differently, loves differently. Viewed from the standpoint of faith, even science looks different. That is because such renewed people have the "mind of Christ" (1 Cor. 2:16); that is to say, they feel, think, will, believe, hope, and love like Christ.

Christians have a view of life, of the origin and purpose of reality and all knowledge, different from that of Muslims or atheists, for example. They do obey the same law of logic as do Hindus and agnostics, for example. For them, 2 + 2 = 4, just as it is for Buddhists and materialists. But the laws of logic and of mathematics are, to them, part of a different world, so to speak; these laws function within a different framework. Many laws in Canada and the United States are the same, or similar, but they function in different countries. Later in this book, we will see more clearly in what respects Christians see the world in a different way. Right now, suffice it to say that if Jesus Christ has renewed your heart through his Word and Spirit, your feeling, thinking, desiring, believing, hoping, and loving are different. You look at the world through different glasses. Your sexual life and your economic life are different, your societal and moral views are different, your science is different, because *you* are different.

This notion as such is nothing exceptional. The difference between a Christian and a non-Christian is not that the former views the world through the "glasses" of faith and the latter does not. This is what many atheists and agnostics would like you to believe, but it is not true. Hindus, Buddhists, Muslims, agnostics, atheists, materialists, spiritualists, evolutionists, postmodernists, New Agers, and everyone else look at the world through their own "glasses" of faith. There is nothing wrong with looking through "glasses" *per se*, because we simply have no other option. In this sense, there is no difference between Christians and all the others. In another sense there *is* a difference. The whole point is that Christians believe that their "glasses" are superior, not because they themselves are superior to others—they are not—but because their God and his Word are superior.

Religious Ground-Motives (2)

As I conclude this chapter, let me come back once more to the phrase "religious ground-motive." The phrase "religious ground-motive" refers to the deepest or most basic motive that drives our hearts, and that therefore is necessarily religious. Note well: we are using the term *ground* to mean *basic*, and the term *motive* to refer to what *motivates* (drives or directs) all our being and doing. Operating from the heart, these ground-motives govern our feelings, our will, our rational deliberations, our social and moral decisions, etc.

Herman Dooyeweerd formulated four such religious ground-motives, which I briefly describe here:

(a) The *matter–form* ground-motive dominated ancient Greek thinking.

(b) The *nature–grace* ground-motive dominated medieval Scholastic thinking.

(c) The *nature–freedom* ground-motive governed, and still governs, humanistic thinking since the time of the Enlightenment.

(d) The Christian ground-motive is that of *creation, fall, and redemption*.

After Dooyeweerd did his work, Christian philosophers have pointed out some weaknesses in this outline. First, topics like matter and form, nature and grace, nature and freedom, and creation, fall, and redemption, can at best be *rational* formulations of what, as a *ground*-motive, necessarily possesses a supra-rational character. In particular, the Christian ground-motive of *creation, fall, and redemption* looks more like a mini-theology—debatable at that (see below)—than like a religious, supra-rational, transcendent *ground*-motive.

In the end, many Christian thinkers would rather say that there can only be two *ground*-motives in the proper sense of the term: what some have called the *anastatic* ground-motive of the regenerated heart enlightened by the Holy Spirit, and the *apostatic* ground-motive of the sinful, unregenerated heart. This latter supra-rational ground-motive comes to expression in several basic pagan rational approaches in Western thinking, such as the matter–form motive (not *ground*-motive) and the nature–freedom motive.

In addition to this, Western thought is characterized by several motives that are of a mixed character, as may be expected in our imperfect world. One example is the medieval nature–grace motive, which is a mixture of Christian and ancient-pagan thinking. Other examples are the several mixtures of Christian and humanistic thinking in the last centuries, blends that we find in the thought systems of Georg W.F. Hegel, Søren Kierkegaard, Friedrich W.J. Schelling, Reinhold Niebuhr, Albert Schweitzer, Paul Ricoeur, and many others.

A truly Christian *ground*-motive is the basic motive that drives the heart on a supra-rational, transcendent level. It is a bit dangerous to try to design a rational formulation for it because, firstly, such a formulation is consequently no *ground*-motive anymore. Secondly, theologians will always keep fighting about the most proper formulation of it—even if they have supplied us with such a formulation at all. Many theologians might like to bring in the notion of the covenant, others would prefer the notion of the kingdom of God, still others choose the Orthodox notion of *theosis* (deification, the realization of the image of God in the believer). This discussion would lead us into the deep waters of theology, so we refrain from it in this philosophical introduction (but see chapter 8). More relevant to our present point is the notion of the two real ground-motives: the anastatic and the apostatic one.

Questions for Review

1. Where and how did Western philosophy begin?

2. What are some implications or results of the preference of Greek philosophers for thinking rather than for seeing?

3. What important idea did Augustine teach about the relation between faith and reason?

4. Explain how philosophy and theology were viewed by Thomas Aquinas and William of Occam.

5. What four solutions do people propose for the relationship between faith and reason?

6. Explain the fifth solution, which emphasizes thinking based on supra-rational faith.

7. What are "religious ground-motives"? Give some examples.

8. Identify and explain these modern philosophical schools: existentialism, New Age, and postmodernism.

9. What does it mean that faith and the human heart are "transcendent," and why is this idea important?

10. Why can human reason never be autonomous, but is always directed by faith, whether true or false?

11. "Biblical faith is not a package of logical beliefs, but primarily a relationship of confidence." How does this affect our Bible reading, church worship, and praying?

12. Explain the four examples of "religious ground-motive" identified by Herman Dooyeweerd. What criticism could be leveled against his view?

Chapter Three

A CHRISTIAN VIEW OF COSMIC REALITY

We have seen that philosophy has two important tasks to accomplish: it has to supply us with a view of reality (cosmology), and with a theory of knowledge (epistemology). Christian philosophy has to accomplish the same thing, by answering the question: What does a Christian view of reality and of knowledge look like?

Let us start with the first task. Of course, not just philosophy but all the special sciences attempt to supply us with a view of reality. The difference is this: the special sciences are always occupied with only a part of cosmic reality. Physicists are occupied with physical phenomena, biologists with life (or biotic) phenomena, linguists with language (or lingual) problems, economists with economic matters, ethicists with moral questions, etc. They never take the whole picture into account; they are not even *supposed* to do that. They look at cosmic reality from one angle only.

With philosophical cosmology it is very different. It does not enter into the fields of the various special sciences, and its contents are not a kind of summary of the special sciences. Rather, philosophy should come up with a kind of general picture, a kind of totality view of cosmic reality (or, ontology) as well as a view of the coherence of all the various special sciences (or, epistemology).

The Coherence of the Special Sciences

Supplying a totality view of the coherence of the various special sciences amounts to investigating how these sciences relate to one another. If each of them investigates a certain group of phenomena, is there a certain sequential order and arrangement in these various groups of phenomena? Let us see.

It is a good idea to start with mathematics because this is a very basic science. Many special sciences are based upon it, certainly all the natural sciences, but mathematics itself does not seem to be based on any other special science. So it has a foundational character.

When you look at it more closely, mathematics turns out to consist of two rather different sciences. Firstly, there is arithmetic, the science of number (the Greek word *arithmos* means "number"); this science includes algebra. Secondly, there is geometry, the science of form. The interesting fact is that, on the one hand, form always presupposes number, because forms—think of geometrical figures—can be measured, that is, expressed in numbers. On the other hand, numbers do not presuppose forms. So arithmetic is basic to geometry, but not the other way around. In other words, we have the arithmetical dimension first, then the geometrical, or as we shall term it, the spacial dimension.

Next, we come to physics. In any case, I cannot see any science coming in between mathematics and physics. In physics, we enter the world of tangible things. Actually, physics, too, consists of two rather different sciences: kinematics, or the science of pure motion, and energetics, or the science of energy. We cannot imagine energy without motion, but we certainly can imagine motion without energy (uniform motion does not need any energy, only changes in uniform motion do). However, we cannot imagine motion without spatial form: motion always has a certain range in space. Of course, space does not presuppose motion—but motion does presuppose space. So we find a clear-cut order: there is the arithmetical dimension first, then the spatial, then the kinematic, then the energetic. There is no possible way in which you can alter this sequential order and arrangement.

Next, we have biology. Again, I cannot see any science between physics and biology. Biology investigates biotic phenomena, and such phenomena always presuppose the physical; there is no (earthly) life without matter. But the physical does not presuppose the biotic; we do have matter without life. So the biotic fits nicely into our scheme: we have the arithmetical first, then the spatial, then the kinematic, then the energetic, then the biotic.

Next, we have psychology. Again, I do not see any science between biology and psychology. Actually, unlike Dooyeweerd, I believe that elementary psychology, too, has two rather different components. On the one hand, we have perception psychology, the science of what people call *sensations* (German: *Empfindungen*; Dutch: *gewaarwordingen*) and perceptions (German: *Wahrnehmungen*; Dutch: *waarnemingen*). On the other hand, there is sensitive psychology, the science of affections, emotions, urges. I believe that the sensitive always presupposes the perceptive—you can hardly have feeling without some kind of perception—but not the other way around: perception as such does not presuppose feeling. However, the perceptive does presuppose the biotic: within cosmic reality, there is no perception without perceptive organs of living beings. So now we can draw the line a little further: we apparently have the arithmetical first, then the spatial, then the kinematic, then the energetic, then the biotic, then the perceptive, then the sensitive.

Notice this beautiful order of the various natural phenomena studied by the various natural sciences—in so far as we can call psychology a natural science too (a matter of debate that we will not pursue here). Instead, let's see if we can draw this line even further.

Humanities

We now come to what in several publications I have called the "spiritive" sciences. ("Spiritive" is a word I have coined.) I would rather not use the word *spiritual*, because that term can better be reserved for religious matters. I could use *mental*, but that word has negative connotations (associated with "mental institutions"). *Spiritive* means that the sciences that we are going to mention next all have to do with the human spirit or mind. They are often called the humanities, that is, sciences that investigate the human phenomenon.

It is much more difficult to find a similar order among the spiritive sciences, but I will do my best. Or to put it more modestly, I will follow in the line of great thinkers such as Dooyeweerd and Vollenhoven, who had already worked this problem out three quarters of a century ago.

I think we can defend the idea that the science of logic comes first. Logic certainly presupposes the biotic, the perceptive, and the sensitive, for logical thinking presupposes a human brain. All the special sciences I will now mention refer to domains in the human mind that all presuppose logic. So in the (presumed) order of the humanities I suppose that logic comes first. To repeat the sequential order and arrangement we found: first, we have the arithmetical, then the spatial, then the kinematic, then the energetic, then the biotic, then the perceptive, then the sensitive, then the logical.

I have to explain the position of the logical a little further because a misunderstanding could easily arise here. Arithmetic, spatiality, kinematics, energetics, biology, perception, and sensitive psychology, *as sciences*, are also inconceivable without logical thinking. Scientific activity always demands logic. But numbers, spatial figures, motions, energies, perceptions, feelings, and biotic phenomena as such do not presuppose the logical. *Thinking* about these matters, as we do in science, does.

With the humanities it is a different matter. Not only as sciences do they presuppose logic—because all sciences do—but the domains they investigate presuppose the logical as well. For instance, not only sociology, as a science, presupposes the logical, but *social life* does too. That is, there are no human social relationships without thinking.

Let us return to the sequential order and arrangement of the special sciences that we are trying to discover. It can be argued that, after logic, the formative sciences come next. That includes historiography, the study of formative power in history, but also the technology sciences, the study of formative power in technique. They all presuppose the logical but not necessarily any one of the subsequent aspects of cosmic reality. However, each of the domains investigated by the subsequent special sciences seems to presuppose formative power. So, we have the arithmetical first, then the spatial, then the kinematic, then the energetic, then the biotic, then the perceptive, then the sensitive, then the logical, then the formative.

Linguistics seems to be next. If we are not mistaken, language phenomena presuppose historical process, but presuppose none of the domains studied in the subsequent sciences.

In this way we move cautiously forward. Thus, social concourse presupposes language, whereas economical processes presuppose social relationships. So, after linguistics, we have sociology, and after sociology, we have economics. Harmony presupposes "economy" in the sense of balance, but not the other way around; so we have economics first, then aesthetics. Justice presupposes harmony, but not the other way around; so we have aesthetics first, then the legal sciences, or the science of jurisprudence. Morals presuppose justice, but not the other way around; so we have jurisprudence first, then ethics, which is the science of morality. And beliefs presuppose morality, not necessarily the other way around; so we have ethics first, then the religious sciences, the science of "pistical" phenomena. *Pistis* is Greek for "faith"; we use the word "pistical" to distinguish it from "religious"; I will explain that below.

Sequential Order and Arrangement

The sequential order and arrangement as I have described it here seems to be debatable at certain points. But let us give this model the benefit of the doubt and let us assume that, indeed, there is a remarkable sequential order and arrangement in cosmic reality. If our considerations are correct, we have the arithmetical first, then the spatial, then the kinematic, then the energetic, then the biotic, then the perceptive, then the sensitive, then the logical, then the formative, then the lingual, then the social, then the economic, then the aesthetic, then the juridical, then the ethical, and finally the pistical.

Please note that in this list I am not talking about sciences but about the domains investigated by the various sciences. This is, so to speak, not an epistemological list, but an ontological one. If our approach is correct, we are asserting that, *within cosmic reality as such*, there is something that we vaguely call "the arithmetical element," or "the energetic," or "the sensitive," or "the social," or "the juridical element," etc. Epistemologically, that is, speaking of the various special sciences, there seems to be a striking sequential order: we find mathematics first, and at the end of the list we find theology. But this sequential order and arrangement corresponds with something of an ontological nature: within cosmic reality we find "the arithmetical" first, and at the end of the list we find "the pistical."

Thus, the epistemological order is a reflection of a certain ontological order. In the latter case, regarding the order from the arithmetical to the pistical, we speak of "aspects" of reality. These aspects certainly have an epistemological character; that is, they are aspects of our knowledge. They represent sixteen windows through which we can look at cosmic reality. We can study our world from an arithmetical, or a perceptive, or a social, or a pistical angle, etc. But they also have an ontological character; I believe they are real aspects of cosmic reality itself. If we are not mistaken, our world is mathematical, and spatial, and so on, and in the end it is also moral and pistical.

We call these aspects *modal* aspects, or *modalities* of reality. The word "mode" comes from the Latin *modus*; in this case it means: a way of being. There seem to be about sixteen modes, that is, sixteen ways things exist and function. Things are arithmetical, spatial, kinematic, energetic, etc. You can also say: things function in the arithmetical modality, the spatial modality, the kinematic, the energetic, etc., modality, or more simply, they function in an arithmetical, spatial, kinematic, energetic, (etc.) way.

Phenomena and Aspects

At this point we have to introduce some more accuracy. What are we actually talking about? I have said that the science of kinematics studies kinematic phenomena, biology studies biotic phenomena, social sciences study social phenomena, and ethics studies moral phenomena. But this is not a very precise way of putting it.

Let us take biology as an example. Biology studies biotic phenomena, but what is that precisely? Is a plant a biotic phenomenon? It seems easy and correct to say that certain biologists study plants. But a plant has many aspects, and most of them are not of any interest at all to biologists as such. Geometry is better equipped than biology to study certain geometrical forms of plants, or of plant parts. Physicists know more than biologists do about the working of molecules in plants. Those who cultivate plants—a formative science—know more than the average biologist does about growing plants. Sociologists and ethical specialists know more than biologists do about the social and moral functions of plants.

Economists know more than biologists do about the market value of certain plants. And theologians know more than biologists as such about the religious significance of plants.

These observations lead to a most interesting conclusion. In a sense, under certain circumstances, *all* special sciences may become interested in plants, *but they are always interested in one single aspect of plants only.* Geometry, physics, psychology, linguistics, sociology, aesthetics, and ethics may all show some interest in (certain) plants, but only in the spatial, the physical, the sensitive, the lingual, the social, the aesthetic, or the moral aspect of them, respectively.

For biologists, the same conclusion is true. Biologists may be very interested in plants but, strictly speaking, only the biotic aspect of plants belongs to their specific field of investigation. We will see that the biotic aspect is the most characteristic aspect of plants, so there is nothing wrong in saying that plants are the primary object of study for biologists. However, it is of great interest to discover that every science at a certain moment may become interested in plants—but always in one specific aspect of plants only, according to the science in view.

Conversely, we can say that there is no subject within cosmic reality in which biologists might not become interested, *because all things have a biotic aspect,* as we will see.

This leads to something that to me is a most fascinating conclusion: mathematics, geometry, kinematics, energetics, biology, perceptive and sensitive psychology, logic, the formative sciences, linguistics, sociology, economics, aesthetics, the juridical sciences, ethics, and theology are all interested in the *whole* of reality, but each of them only from a certain aspect, a certain angle, namely, the arithmetical, the spatial, the kinematic, the energetic, the biotic, the perceptive, the sensitive, the logical, the formative, the lingual, the social, the economic, the aesthetic, the juridical, the ethical, and the pistical viewpoint, respectively.

Of course, there are many more sciences than the ones I have enumerated, but each of these other sciences seems to be a kind of mixture of the sciences mentioned, or a kind of applied science. For instance, astronomy is nothing but the physics of celestial bodies. Geography is the study of the physical and the social aspects of the earth (surface). Engineering and computer sciences are physics applied within technology. Chemistry has been called the physics of the outer orbits of the electrons (because only these are involved in chemical reactions). Medical sciences are biology applied to sick people. Pharmaceutics is physics and biology applied to the development of medicines. Education sciences are psychology and sociology applied to pupils and students.

I think you would have a hard time finding any other basic aspect than the sixteen I mentioned above. Of course, this is not a fixed number; the system is always open to further investigation. In theory, it is always possible that a new modal aspect is identified. But for the time being, let us assume these sixteen aspects to be comprehensively adequate.

Sixteen Modal Aspects?

Of course, the question is not only whether there might not be *more* than these sixteen modal aspects, but also whether we have perhaps distinguished *too many* of them. How can we be sure that some of these modal aspects could not be reduced to one of the other aspects? Actually, it was through this question that Herman Dooyeweerd was confronted with the issue of "modal aspects." He was a young professor of the philosophy of law (German: *Rechtsphilosophie*, Dutch: *rechtsfilosofie*), and came across the fact that many philosophers of law in the past had tried to reduce the notion of "what is right" (Latin: *ius*, as in "justice," "jurisprudence"; German: *Recht*, Dutch: *recht*) to other sciences. Some said that what is "right" is basically an evolutionary idea, an evolutionary product; it is nothing but biotic. Others claimed that the term "right" is basically a sensitive term; that is, what we experience as "right" is nothing but a psychical phenomenon (German: *Rechtsgefühl*, Dutch: *rechtsgevoel*). Still others asserted that "right" is basically a moral matter; that is, it is exclusively ethical.

This tendency is quite understandable. It can be explained from the human inclination to reduce the complex to the simple. It would be very convenient if, in the enormous variety of phenomena, we could distinguish one, or a few, general principles. Scientists are trying to do this all the time. It is when people exaggerate such simplification processes that we speak of *reductionism*; this term refers to the assertion that everything is "nothing but this" or "nothing but that." This is sometimes mockingly called "nothing-but-ism."

For instance, some say that everything is basically material (physicalism, materialism). In the end, all phenomena we know can be reduced to the properties of atoms and molecules, they claim. In fact, if this were true, it would make things a lot simpler. The problem is that others have argued with the same fervor that everything is basically evolutionary (evolutionism): everything is a product of an evolutionary process. Or that everything is spiritual (spiritualism): everything is basically "mind"; matter is "compressed mind," etc. Or that everything is logic, which claims that "reason" (*logos*) is the basis of the whole cosmos (rationalism). Or that our whole culture is rooted in social relationships (socialism), or in economic relationships (Marxism), etc. All these "everything-is-nothing-but"-isms—and there are many more—cannot be right at the same time.

In itself, it is an interesting phenomenon that apparently every aspect of reality has been absolutized at some time in history. "Absolutizing" here means: making it absolute, making it the one and only thing to which all other things can be reduced. Let me give you some examples.

Pythagoras and his followers said, "Everything is number," thus absolutizing the arithmetical aspect.

René Descartes distinguished between the *res cogitans* (the "thinking thing"), that is, the human mind, and the *res extensa* (the "extended thing"), that is, the rest of reality. He reduced the latter part of reality to "extension," a spatial notion, as if that were the most important aspect of material things. So he absolutized the spatial aspect.

Galileo Galilei tried to reduce material reality to motion, so he tended to absolutize the kinematic aspect.

Materialists say that everything is nothing but matter, thus absolutizing the energetic aspect. Remember, matter is "compressed energy."

Evolutionists say that everything is the product of a biotic evolution, thus absolutizing the biotic aspect.

George Berkeley said, *esse est percipi*, "being is being perceived," thus absolutizing the perceptive aspect.

Psychologists like Sigmund Freud reduced all spiritual life to the psychical, thus absolutizing the sensitive aspect.

Heraclitus made the *Logos* ("Reason") the fundamental principle within reality, thus absolutizing the logical aspect.

Historicism is a feature of several philosophical schools that see all culture as nothing but products of historical development, thus absolutizing the formative aspect.

Analytic philosophy tends to reduce philosophical problems to linguistic problems, thus absolutizing the lingual aspect.

Socialism reduces all culture to social relationships, especially to the importance of the state, thus absolutizing the social aspect.

Karl Marx reduced all human culture to economic relationships, thus absolutizing the economic aspect.

The Renaissance and the Romantic movement tended to reduce all culture to notions of harmony and beauty, thus absolutizing the aesthetic aspect.

Immanuel Kant reduced all spiritual life to ethics, thus absolutizing the moral aspect.

And Christian movements such as pietism have the tendency to reduce everything to the religious aspects of life—"religion" here in the sense of prayer, praise, and preaching—thus absolutizing the pistical aspect of cosmic reality. In a sense, we are always religious people in that we always think, speak, and act *coram Deo*, "before God," for the glory or the dishonor of his name. But that does not mean that all our thoughts, words, and actions are pistical in character. Also when we are constructing bridges, or writing literature, or socializing, or buying and selling, or painting, or passing legislation, we do these things as standing before God—or our idols—that is, we do these things as religious people. We are always religious, but that does not mean we are thereby always acting pistically.

Idolatry

As you can see, reductionism is quite a common phenomenon! Apart from the legal sciences, I have mentioned *all* the special sciences. Please note again, reduction may be a good thing. If you can reduce a complex part of reality to some simple explanatory principles, you have done an important job. In fact, as I said, this is an essential part of all scientific activity. But you can take this sort of reductionism too far. If so many different sciences all say, "Actually, everything is nothing but mathematics (or physics, or logic, or economy, etc.)," this cannot be true. All these claims contradict and exclude one another. Indeed, I believe *they are all wrong*.

Interestingly, however, there is a kernel of truth in all these "nothing-but-isms." All things do have an arithmetical aspect! So you can easily imagine someone saying, "Everything is number." But all things have an energetic aspect as well. So you can understand someone saying, "Everything is energy (or matter, for that matter)." All things also have a logical aspect. So you can see why certain people consider rationalism to be the all-encompassing ideology. All things also have an economic aspect. So you can see why certain people think that all culture is nothing but the elaboration of economic principles.

Because *all* things exhibit *all* sixteen modal aspects we have mentioned, we can easily imagine how every aspect can be absolutized in some way or another. All these attempts equally have a kernel of truth—and in the end, they are all equally false. So why do people keep absolutizing some aspect of cosmic reality? Why this strong tendency in the human mind? Let me explain.

You know from the Bible what idolatry is. Idolatry means worshipping not the Creator but some creature: the sun, the moon, the planets, certain trees, certain animals, rocks, rivers, you name it. This is what the apostle Paul says: "Although they claimed to be wise, they became fools and exchanged the glory of the immortal God for images made to look like mortal human beings and birds and animals and reptiles" (Rom. 1:22-23). This is what idolatry basically is: worshipping some creature instead of the Creator.

Now, I think that worshipping not some specific creature but some "principle" within creation amounts to the same thing. It is still idolatry. Take someone who claims that all properties of living beings, and even of thinking beings, can be reduced to the properties of matter and energy; in brief: "everything is matter." We call him or her a materialist, or a physicalist, someone who is absolutizing the energetic aspect of cosmic reality. Christians say that the explanatory principle for reality is its Creator, God. Materialists say that the explaining principle for reality is something within reality itself, namely matter. He may not literally "worship" matter, but at least he is not far from worshipping materialism. Materialism is to him what my Christian faith is to me. Every ideology that functions as some Ultimate Ground in which Man places his ultimate confidence is basically religious, as I have tried to show (chapter 2). It is the same with spiritualism ("Everything can be reduced to the properties of the spiritual"), rationalism, socialism, Marxist economism, and all the other -isms I have mentioned. We call them nothing-but-isms because they claim that "everything is nothing-but-this" or "nothing-but-that."

Why does a sound Christian philosophy *not* exhibit this tendency of trying to reduce all things to one principle ("monism") or perhaps two principles ("dualism")? Because Christian philosophy realizes that we cannot begin to understand cosmic reality by reducing it to one or two of its modal aspects, but by "reducing" it to its origin, the Creator. This was what dawned upon the mind of Herman Dooyeweerd and others: Do not try to reduce the various modal aspects of cosmic reality to each other, but treat all these aspects as equal, one next to the other, as aspects with which God has equipped his creation. Justice—Dooyeweerd's subject—is not a biotic thing, it is not a psychical thing, it is not a logical thing, it is not an ethical thing. Justice is simply *justice*. It represents a cosmic aspect of its own, one that cannot be reduced to any other aspect whatsoever.

Please note: *matters* of justice, such as tribunals and verdicts, do have a biotic, a psychical, a logical, and an ethical aspect. But they are *typified* or *characterized* by the juridical aspect, and nothing else. Of course, they have a biotic and a psychical aspect: if there were no living, sensitive beings, then the notion of justice within our cosmic reality would make no sense. And of course, they have a logical aspect: we can rationally argue about what is justice and what is not justice, how just a certain act of justice is, etc. But that does not make a verdict a rational thing, as rationalism might easily conclude. No, it is a juridical thing, with a rational (and a physical, and a social, and an economic, and an ethical, and a pistical) aspect. The juridical does not have to be explained from other modal aspects. It is to be explained from the Creator, who gave all things within the cosmos a juridical aspect (what this means exactly, I will explain in more detail below).

Properties of Modal Aspects

This is why I claim that the theory of the modal aspects is a characteristic feature of a truly Christian philosophy. This philosophy can withstand the temptation of idolatrously reducing aspects to other aspects because it knows of the Creator. It is able to leave the modal aspects alone, to emphatically state their equality, and to maintain their position alongside each other.

By the way, it is not very easy to understand the notion of a "modal aspect" correctly. Particularly in the beginning, students often confuse modal aspects with concrete things or certain states of affairs. Somebody once suggested that the sexual should also be recognized as a modal aspect. He did not see that sexuality is not on the "aspect-side" but on the "thing-side" of reality. It is an "event" that, *like all events*, functions in *all* sixteen modal aspects of reality. Sexuality has an obvious biotic aspect (it involves reproductive organs, hormones, etc.), a psychical aspect (it involves sensations and strong emotions). It also has a logical aspect (you can think about it), a social aspect (it involves relationships between people), a juridical aspect (some forms of sexual expression are legal, while others, like rape, are not), and an ethical aspect (some forms of sexual expression are moral, while others are not). Sexuality even has a historical aspect (sexual habits change with time), an economic aspect (there is such a horrible thing as a "sex industry"), an aesthetic aspect (some sexual habits are perversions, others are harmonious), and a pistical aspect (you can never ever sever sexuality from your beliefs).

In conclusion: modal aspects as such are not themselves phenomena but always only *aspects* of phenomena. Aspects are ways things are (to put it ontologically): they are arithmetical, spatial, etc. Aspects are also ways we can view things (to put it epistemologically): they can be viewed from an arithmetical angle, a geometrical angle, etc.

Of course, the confusing thing is that there *are* physical, biotic, economic phenomena, etc. What is the difference between the physical aspect and a physical phenomenon? A phenomenon is "thing-like," and as such is always *qualified* by the physical, the biotic, or the economic aspect, or whatever aspect it may be. But it is equally true that each of these phenomena functions in *all* sixteen modal aspects of cosmic reality. For instance, economic phenomena are qualified by the economic aspect; that is the aspect that expresses their "quality" (Latin *qualitas*, their "being thus-and-so"). But economic phenomena also have a psychical, a rational, a historical, a social aspect, etc.

I repeat: *all things* (lifeless things, plants, animals, humans), *events, and states of affairs always function in all sixteen modal aspects.* But they are usually *qualified*, or characterized, by one or two of these aspects (I will return to this latter point in chapter 5). That may help you to keep distinguishing between things and aspects. Things always function in all sixteen modal aspects, whereas a modal aspect is just one of these sixteen. If this is not yet entirely clear to you, I recommend that you read the preceding paragraphs again, until you have a good idea of what modal aspects are all about, and what they are not.

Historical Note

One important stimulus that helped Dooyeweerd to develop his theory of the modal aspects is worth mentioning. One of the men who influenced the young Dooyeweerd most was Abraham Kuyper (1837-1920), a pastor, theologian, journalist and politician; he was prime minister of the Netherlands from 1901 to 1905. Kuyper developed the principle of *sphere sovereignty*. Basically, he wanted to claim that the church should rule over the state, nor should the state rule over the church, but that each is relatively sovereign within its own sphere or domain of activity. Do not interfere with each other's sphere! The state is there to maintain public justice, and thus creates the outward conditions under which churches can operate, but does not meddle in the internal affairs of churches. The same holds for marriages, families, associations, political parties, etc.: each is sovereign within its own sphere.

Dooyeweerd adopted this very fruitful idea, and applied it to his theory of the modal aspects. Each of these aspects is sovereign within its own sphere, that is, no modality rules over any of the other ones, and no modality can be reduced to any of the other modalities. Each modal aspect knows its own specific laws, laws that again are irreducible to the laws of the other aspects. Here we meet with another term that has played an important role in the Reformed tradition: *law*. Reformed theologians had paid much attention to the creational ordinances God had instituted for the various parts of cosmic reality. Dooyeweerd made this notion fruitful within philosophy by distinguishing the laws characterizing the various modal aspects. This notion of *law* is so important that it is the subject of the next chapter.

Finally: Time

Time is a complex philosophical subject. Already in everyday language the term *time* has many meanings. Here are some phrases we use. It's time. Time flies. Time is up. A long time ago. In the meantime. Time heals all wounds. Time will teach you. Time will tell. It's a matter of time. You're wasting your time. Working against time. Ahead of time. At one time. Once upon a time. At times. Keeping time. Try to find out for yourself how many different meanings the word *time* has in all these different sayings!

Christian thinkers have always thought about time in relation to God and to eternity. One of these questions is whether God exists beyond time, and is thus timeless, or whether he is, in some way or another, within time as we know it, or within some divine kind of time. If we speak of physical time, the time of clocks, which is closely linked with matter, then God cannot be within time. He does pervade the cosmos—God is omnipresent—but he is not part of it; he is beyond it. He transcends all matter that he himself created, and thus also time as it is linked with the material world. However, this does not necessarily imply that God is timeless. To put it more strongly: the Bible can speak of God only in terms derived from our own *temporal* world. But these terms should not be taken in a strictly physical sense but in a pistical sense; they are metaphorical in nature. Theological opinions differ widely on the question whether God is temporally everlasting, or timelessly eternal, but the latter notion has fewer and fewer adherents.

Let us leave this matter of God's alleged (supra)temporality to the theologians, and limit ourselves to philosophical questions pertaining to time and the cosmos. Just as theology makes its contribution to our thinking about time, physics does the same thing. Physicists see time and matter as solidly coupled. This means that physical time began at the moment the universe (at least as we know it today) began. This notion goes back already to the church father Augustine, but today physicists add a number of considerations about which Augustine could not have had the slightest idea. For instance, it is assumed that in a black hole, not only matter but also time vanishes. That means there could be places in the universe where there is no time anymore. And Albert Einstein's theory of relativity implies that someone traveling through the universe at the speed of light comes back in a different time frame. Even in the case of speeds much lower than that of light, such as with satellites, differences of milliseconds have already been measured. Time is neither independent of matter, nor a static notion.

Temporal Modalities

Time has been created, time and the created cosmos belong together, and the modal aspects are aspects of the temporal cosmos. If this is so, this seems to suggest that the modal aspects could also be called *temporal* aspects in the sense of aspects of our temporal reality.

The young Dooyeweerd, and others as well, played with the idea that cosmic time itself could be a modal aspect. In that case, it might be linked with the kinematic aspect, or be assigned as a distinct modality coming before the arithmetical aspect. None of these suggestions has turned out to be satisfactory though. If time were a separate modality, then the other modalities might be thought of as presupposing this time modality, but they would not themselves be temporal in character. That would be just as unacceptable as if someone were to suggest there is some cosmic modality—as if the other modalities were not cosmic in nature.

Moreover, if time were a separate modality, try to imagine what could be the kernel or essence of this modal aspect, just as we have kernels for all the other modalities. And within this assumed time modality, what could be the analogies with other modalities (see chapter 4 below, about analogies)? No, this does not seem to be a fruitful path to take. Other Christian philosophers have rejected the very notion of some cosmic time that would express itself within all the various modal aspects in its own specific way. The present elementary introduction to Christian philosophy is not the appropriate place to explain and expand on all these discussions.

Let me just state that if we do adopt this notion of some kind of cosmic time expressing itself within the various modal aspects, this seems to be a fruitful approach:

Arithmetical: Time comes to expression in the numerical succession. Typically temporal terms like "before" and "after" make sense in this succession: 2 comes after 1, and before 3.

Spatial: Time seems to manifest itself here particularly in the notion of simultaneity, that is, "being-at-the-same-time." Geometrical figures, and any shapes in the cosmos, can exist only in the simultaneous existence of their various geometrical parts.

Kinematic: Time linked with motion; no motion exists without physical time.

Energetic: Time linked with energetic processes, which cannot exist without physical time, either. This is what we call "clock-time," time as measured and indicated by clocks.

Biotic: Time linked with biotic processes such as birth, maturation, blossoming, death, or with the four seasons, or "biological (more precisely, biotic] clocks."

Perceptive: Time linked with sensations and perceptions; the perceptive experience of time.

Sensitive: Felt time as distinct from physical time, the emotional experience of time (time with the dentist or time spent with your beloved).

Logical: This is the "before" and "after" in arguments: conclusions "follow from" premises, never the other way around.

Formative: Historical developments or periods, historic moments and the like, not measured with clocks but according to historical criteria.

Lingual: Think of the grammatical tenses, locating events in time, be they in the past, the present, or the future.

Social: Think of priority (before-ness) in social relationships ("ladies first"), or in street traffic; priority was originally a temporal term.

Economic: "Save time!" The notion of monetary interest is an interesting example. It refers to a fee paid by the borrower of money (or of other assets) to the owner as a reward for the use of it, the size of the fee being determined by the time period during which the money is borrowed. "Time is money!"

Aesthetic: Think of the attention paid in novels to historical events. Some bulky novels describe just one day or a few days, others cover long historical epochs.

Juridical: Prison penalties link the time of imprisonment with the seriousness of the crime committed. Also think of laws with retroactive force, or crimes that can be punished only within a certain span of time.

Ethical: The blossoming of love needs time; in other cases, time may be running out for doing good. There is a time to do the right thing (Eccl. 3:1-8).

Pistical: The alternation of festival days (holy days) and common days, and especially: that which is beyond time, breaking through into our cosmic reality (divine revelation).

I have not given you this list with the intention of ending all discussion. On the contrary, on a number of points quite some battles have been waged that are still going on. For instance, do the words *before* and *after* always imply time? Or with respect to the higher modal aspects, in a certain sense is not physical time always presupposed? I mention these as examples of how philosophy is never finished but is always under development. Here is something to which you yourself could make a contribution. Don't swallow everything I tell you! That would not be the proper evaluative philosophical attitude.

Questions for Review

1. List, and briefly describe, each of the special sciences discussed in the section "The Coherence of Special Sciences."

2. List, and briefly describe, each of the "spiritive sciences" discussed in the section "Humanities."

3. Explain what is meant by the phrase "modal aspects."

4. What do the terms "absolutizing" and "reductionism" mean, and how do they relate to what the Bible teaches about idolatry?

5. In what sense could a sound Christian philosophy avoid the dangers identified in Question 4?

6. Explain the difference between *things* and *aspects* of things.

7. How does Dooyeweerd's theory of modal aspects fit with Abraham Kuyper's idea of sphere sovereignty?

8. Explain the characteristics of a "modal aspect" of the cosmos. How can you identify one as such?

9. In the light of Question 8, how do you feel about the list of modal aspects as given in this chapter? Do you wonder whether some of them are modalities at all, or whether some should not be added to the list? Explain.

10. Explain, in terms of each modality, why the aspect of time is not a distinct cosmic modality, but rather expresses itself within each of these cosmic modalities?

Chapter Four

COSMIC REALITY AND GOD'S LAW

In the previous chapter, we have made a beginning with our philosophical analysis of cosmic reality. We have distinguished sixteen modal aspects, and have discovered that *all* lifeless things, plants, animals, humans, events, and states of affairs function in *all* modal aspects, but are *qualified*, or *characterized*, by one, or perhaps two, of these aspects.

Law-Spheres

There is another way Dooyeweerd describes the modal aspects, namely, with the phrase *law-spheres*. What does that mean? You remember what I said about the great pioneers of the modern natural sciences: they learned to believe in a fixed law-order, or world order. The cosmos is an ordered world because God laid this order within it. This order is a law-order, that is, it consists of a number of laws that God has instituted for cosmic reality. The Bible is replete with references to this will of God, his laws, his ordinances, to which he has subjected the cosmos (e.g., Job 38:33; Pss. 119:89, 91; 148:6, 8; Isa. 45:12; Jer. 31:35; 33:25; Rev. 4:11). The founders of modern science knew about the world order and about these fixed laws because they knew the *Lawgiver*, the God of the Bible.

This notion of law is of the utmost importance in Christian philosophy. Actually, Herman Dooyeweerd originally called his philosophy the "Philosophy of the Law Idea." Anglo-Saxon translators have rendered this as the "Cosmonomic Philosophy," that is, the idea of the law (Greek: *nomos*) as foundational for the cosmos. All things within cosmic reality are subject to the laws that the Creator has instituted for them.

Of course, other philosophers and scientists also know about natural laws. In a sense, you could even define all philosophy and science as attempts to unveil the law-order that rules this cosmos. But these other philosophers and scientists have no idea about what the origin of this law-order might be. Even the philosopher of Jewish descent, Karl Popper, whom I mentioned before, admits that, to him, the origin of the law-order is a mystery. If he had studied the Hebrew Bible, I think he would have found the answer!

No philosopher or scientist can claim that the world's law-order might be a by-product of some evolutionary process, because every one believes that the law-order of cosmic reality is absolutely constant, at all times and at all places in the universe. We call this the *principle of uniformity*. We would not even be able to study the history of the earth and of the living world if we had to assume that natural laws are different now than they were thousands—or if you like, millions—of years ago. Only Christians (and Jews and Muslims) have an explanation for this: the constant law-order was created by God. He has created the ordered world that is placed under this world order, and he has instituted the world order that operates in this ordered world (Hendrik Hart).

The ordered world and the world order are, so to speak, two sides of the same created cosmic reality. The ordered world is made up of *facts* (lifeless things, plants, animals, humans), including events and states of affairs. The world order is made up of *laws* that hold for all these things, events, and states of affairs. The ordered world is on the *factual side* (or *subject-side*) of reality, while the world order is on the *law-side* of reality.

Now the interesting point is that you find this double-sidedness within the modal aspects as well. On the one hand, the aspects refer to the factual matters of which they are aspects. On the other hand, the aspects comprise certain laws that are typical of these aspects and that hold for the factual matters *of which* they are aspects. Put in simpler terms, there are modally qualified *facts*, and there are modal *laws* that hold for these facts. The laws govern the facts, the facts are under the laws.

Let me give you some examples, and you will more easily understand what I mean.

There are arithmetical things, namely, numbers (bear with me as I call them "things" for a moment), and there are arithmetical laws that hold for numbers. These are laws like 2 + 2 = 4, a law we learn already in elementary school.

There are spatial "things," geometrical figures like circles and cubes, and there are geometrical laws that hold for these "things," like Pythagoras' Theorem: $a^2 + b^2 = c^2$.

There are physical things—actually, *all* tangible things are physical things—and physical laws that hold for them, such as the laws of electromagnetism and of gravity.

There are biotic things, namely, all living beings, and biotic laws that hold for them, such as the laws of genetics.

There are logical things, namely, human beings, and logical laws that hold for them, such as the laws that govern so-called syllogisms (miniature arguments).

There are economic things, namely, human beings again, and economic laws that hold for them, such as the law of supply and demand.

Are you getting the point? Every modal aspect, or law-sphere, has its own characteristic laws that you do not find in any other aspect. If they are carefully investigated and explained, it should be impossible to reduce them to laws of other law-spheres. Just as modal aspects cannot be reduced to one another, so too modal laws cannot be reduced to one another.

Natural Laws and Norms

Looking at the sixteen law-spheres again, (p. 55-57) you may notice that the laws belonging to the lower modal aspects are different in character from the laws in the higher modal aspects. In the lower law-spheres we have to do with *natural laws;* in the higher law-spheres we have to do with *spiritive norms.* In simple terms the difference is this: natural laws tell us what is, whereas norms tell us what ought to be. For instance, one natural law is the following: iron expands when heated. This law does not stipulate that iron ought to expand when heated, but it simply describes that it does so, under all circumstances. This is a law that cannot be disobeyed, whereas norms can be disobeyed. Whenever you heat iron, it will expand. There is no choice, and there are no exceptions. If you slip from a roof, you cannot decide what you ought to do. There is no option; you will fall, because that is what the law of gravity prescribes. (What you ought to do, is try grabbing the roof gutter—but that does not change the laws of gravity as such.)

With spiritive norms it is essentially different; they are not natural laws. If you want to think correctly, you ought to follow the laws of logic, but you can also disobey them and commit a thinking error or mistake. You do have a choice here. If you want to construct something correctly, you ought to follow formative (in this case, technical) laws, but you can also choose to ignore them. It is unwise, but you can do it; it is up to you. There are also historical norms, like the norm of historical continuity, that is, the uninterrupted progress of cultural development. This implies following a road between traditionalism and reactionism on the one hand, and revolutionism on the other. Both reactionism and revolutionism involve disobedience to God-given norms.

If you want to write English correctly—which I, as a Dutchman, try to do as well as I can—you ought to follow many lingual (in this case, grammatical and orthographical) laws. If you disobey them, you make linguistic mistakes (or errors); you write "bad" English.

If, in social concourse, you want to behave in a correct way, you ought to follow certain social norms, that is, norms that describe how people should associate with other people. Such norms may differ from society to society, and from time to time, but there clearly seem to be certain ground-patterns in social relationships that are universal.

If, in your economic actions, you want to behave in a correct way, you ought to follow economic norms. A clear example is this: you must "cut your coat according to your cloth." This proverb means: Don't spend more than you earn, or you will get yourself into financial trouble. Another example is: you have to invest in your business before you can make money from it. That is not a matter of taste or choice; it is a norm that is given with economic reality. I even dare to say: it is a norm that the Creator has laid within creation, just like logical, historical, lingual, social, aesthetic, juridical, ethical, and pistical norms. They are not inventions of Man. At least, this is a matter that has to be constantly investigated in order to distinguish temporary, man-made norms from permanent, God-given norms.

Again, it is Christian philosophers who easily accept such a thing as permanent, God-given norms, whereas secular philosophers will always be tempted to argue such spiritive norms away, to reduce them to natural laws, or to consider them as arbitrary, man-made. In short, they are not able, or not prepared, to recognize the *creational* character of permanent, universal norms.

For instance, when it comes to aesthetics, many people say, *De gustibus non est disputandum*, which means: "There is no arguing about matters of taste." To a certain extent this is true, of course. Some prefer classical music, others pop music; some prefer Renaissance painting, others impressionist painting. But every expert in the visual arts or in musicology can give you clues as to how to distinguish between good and bad art, good and bad music. What you find "beautiful," what "touches" you, is largely a matter of taste; that is, a matter of the kind of person you are and the way you have been trained. But painting or music of high or low quality is definitely a matter of expertise. There *are* aesthetic norms! There is impressionist painting of high quality and of poor quality. There is pop music of high quality and of poor quality. If you prefer visual arts or music of poor quality, the experts will tell you that your taste has not been very well cultivated. It is like claiming that French fries and popcorn are the tastiest food you've ever eaten!

Interestingly, there is an easy way to illustrate the difference between natural laws, which tell us what is, and spiritive norms, which tell us what *ought to be*. I refer to the fact that words like "unphysical" or "aphysical" (or "unbiotic," or "ageometrical," etc.) do not exist, but words like "illogical," "ahistorical," "asocial," "uneconomic," "unaesthetic," "unrighteous," "unethical" (or "immoral"), and "unbelieving" do exist. That is, you cannot act in an "unphysical" way, for instance, by refusing to obey the law of gravity. This law works under all circumstances. However, you can definitely think "illogically," that is, by disobeying logical norms. You can behave in an asocial, unaesthetic, unrighteous, or an immoral, or an unbelieving way, that is, by disobeying social, aesthetic, juridical, ethical, or pistical norms, respectively. Injustice, immorality, and unbelief do exist. But unarithmetical or unkinematic behavior does not exist; the terms I use here do not even exist. So you see, even in language we are aware of the distinction between natural laws and spiritive norms.

Discovering Laws and Norms

Nowhere in the Bible will you find a complete set of the norms that belong to the various law-spheres. There is no exposition of logical, historical, lingual, social, economic, or aesthetic norms in Scripture. Only when we come to the highest law-spheres do we find that the Bible touches upon the norms belonging to them because they directly affect our daily life of faith. The Bible definitely has a lot to say about juridical, ethical, and pistical norms; in biblical terms, it speaks about the laws of righteousness, of moral love, and of belief in God, and concomitantly, also about unrighteousness, lack of human love, immorality in the broadest sense, unbelief or lack of confidence in God, etc.

However, in the Bible all these laws, and the offences against them, are viewed from the standpoint of faith. The Bible is not interested in a systematic treatment of these various norms as an end in itself. It *is* interested in good and bad behavior before God and our fellowmen. But even when it comes to juridical, ethical, and pistical norms, the Bible does not clearly distinguish between them, because it is not interested in the theory of the modal aspects lying behind the distinction between these norms. Scripture is not interested in *any* theory as such. It is we, philosophers and scientists studying cosmic reality, who come up with a theory of modalities or law-spheres and of the various laws and norms associated with them. In this way, we learn to distinguish between juridical, ethical, and pistical norms, and all the other spiritive norms.

The norms were there all the time, hidden under the surface of God's creation. It is Man who has the task of identifying them, of formulating them in a proper way, and clearly distinguishing between them. As a good philosopher, he or she has to do so in a critical way, always open to new insights, new formulations, and new distinctions. For instance, norms might have been identified that, at a later stage, turn out to be no universal norms at all, but just culturally bound human standards.

This is an important point. On the one hand, Christian philosophy is convinced that the natural laws and spiritive norms identified so far have at least something to do with the nature of cosmic reality as such. They are no mere inventions, but to a certain extent are supposed to account for true states of affairs within creation. On the other hand, our knowledge of these laws and norms is always preliminary, always open to criticism and to further philosophical and scientific investigation. (Reflect on your own about the fact that here again we are encountering the difference between the ontological and the epistemological.)

Subject-Functions

By now, an important question might have crossed your mind. I said that all things, events, and states of affairs function in *all* modal aspects. But, you may ask, how can that be? A plant functions in the energetic and the biotic aspects. Of course it does, for it is subject to the energetic and biotic laws of cosmic reality. But how can we say that a plant also functions in, for instance, the logical and the ethical aspects? A plant cannot think and has no moral values, you may argue.

You are right. But plants do function in the logical and ethical (and psychical, and economic, and aesthetic, etc.) life of human beings! To show what I mean, I have to explain to you the difference between *subjects* and *objects*. This is a well-known matter in philosophical thinking. Usually, philosophers have considered themselves as "(knowing) subjects," and cosmic reality around them as consisting of "(knowing) objects." In other words, Man is the one who knows, and things around him are the things to be known. In this way, the distinction between subjects and objects is primarily an epistemological one, i.e. a matter of knowing. But subjects and objects are also ontological notions; they tell us a little bit about the way things function within reality.

Here again, the notion of the divine law-order is of vital importance. I may view a certain thing as an object that I want to know. But I have to remember that this object is, first of all, itself *subject*—notice that I'm using a verbal adjective here—to the laws of God. I will even never really know that object if I do not primarily recognize the way it is subject to God's laws. Let me give you some examples.

Numbers are subject to—that is, numbers obey—arithmetical laws only; in other words, they function as subjects, or have subject-functions, in the arithmetical modality, but in none of the higher modalities. They are not subject to the laws of geometry, of motion, of energy, etc.

Geometrical figures are subject to arithmetical *and* spatial laws; in other words, they function as subjects, or have subject-functions, in the arithmetical modality—you can make calculations about them—and in the spatial modality: they obey the laws of the spatial mode.

Motions are subject to arithmetical *and* spatial and kinematic laws; in other words, they function as subjects, or have subject-functions, in the arithmetical—you can make calculations about them—*and* in the spatial—they follow a certain range within the spacial order—*and* in the kinematic modality: they obey the laws of motion.

Material things are subject to arithmetical *and* spatial *and* kinematic *and* energetic laws; in other words, they function as subjects, or have subject-functions, in the arithmetical—you can make calculations about them—*and* in the spatial—e.g., they have shapes—*and* in the kinematic—they obey the laws of motion—*and* in the energetic modality: for instance, they obey the laws of electrodynamics and gravity.

In the same way, plants are subject to arithmetical *and* spatial *and* kinematic *and* energetic *and* biotic laws. Lower animals are subject to arithmetical *and* spatial *and* kinematic *and* energetic *and* biotic *and* perceptive laws. Higher animals are subject to arithmetical *and* spatial *and* kinematic *and* energetic *and* biotic *and* perceptive *and* sensitive laws.

Last but not least, humans are subject to *all* modal laws; in other words, they function as subjects, or have subject-functions, in *all* modal aspects: they can think, form, speak, socialize, buy and sell, behave in an (un)righteous, an (im)moral), and an (un)believing way.

Object-Functions

Now we touch upon the crux of the matter. The profound point is that, for instance, plants do function in the higher modalities, too; however, they do so not as subjects but as objects. They cannot feel—they are not sensitive subjects—but they do function as objects in the life of animals (think of plants in an animal's natural habitat or plant materials in a bird's nest) and humans (e.g., plants decorating their yards). We express this fact as follows: plants have "object-functions" in all the modal functions that follow after the biotic modality.

Plants cannot think, for they are not logical *subjects*. But they can be logical *objects* in that humans can think about them. In other words: they have logical object-functions. When we call things "(knowing) objects," that is, objects of a knowing subject, this is in fact the very same thing. Epistemology is sometimes called the special philosophy (*vakfilosofie*) of logic (Andree Troost).

Plants cannot cultivate, for they are not formative *subjects*. But they can be formative *objects* in that humans can cultivate them. In other words, they have formative object-functions.

Plants cannot name things, for they are not lingual *subjects*. But they can be lingual *objects* in that humans can give them names. In other words, they have lingual object-functions.

Plants are not social *subjects*; if we say that many plants "like" to live together, that is only an anthropomorphism (speaking about them as if they were like humans). But plants can be social *objects* in that they function within human social life (e.g., city parks). In other words, they have social object-functions.

Plants cannot buy and sell, for they are not economic *subjects*. But they can be economic *objects* in that humans can buy and sell them. In other words, they have economic object-functions.

Plants have no taste for harmony and beauty, for they are not aesthetic *subjects*. But they can be aesthetic *objects* in that humans attach more or less aesthetic value to them. In other words, they have aesthetic object-functions.

Plants have no sense of justice, for they are not juridical *subjects*. But they can be juridical *objects* in that humans can own or steal them. In other words, they have juridical object-functions.

Plants have no morals, for they are not ethical *subjects*. But they can be ethical *objects* in that humans can use them in their moral life (e.g., if you want to apologize to a friend). In other words, they have ethical object-functions.

Plants cannot believe, for they are not pistical *subjects*. But they can be pistical *objects* in that they can play a role in human religious life (think of the meaning of flowers and trees in the Bible, or in pagan idolatry). In other words, they have pistical object-functions.

Again, this is something you have to understand carefully. We can truly say that *all* things function in *all* modal aspects because we distinguish between subject-functions and object-functions. Elephants have subject-functions in the arithmetical, the spatial, the kinematic, the energetic, the biotic, the perceptive, and the sensitive modalities. They have object-functions in the logical, the formative, the lingual, the social, the economic, the aesthetic, the juridical, the ethical, and the pistical modalities.

Four Additional Remarks

1. Object-functions are not always *activated*; they may remain *latent*. For instance, the object-functions of a stone on the moon, or on the ocean floor, are activated only if and when humans take hold of them and use them, for example, for scientific investigation. Straws and dead leaves lie in the meadow or in the forest with latent sensitive object-functions. The moment a bird comes and picks them up in order to build its nest with them, these object-functions are activated.

2. Humans are the only beings that have no object-functions; they function as subjects in all sixteen modal aspects. They obtain object-functions only if they are dehumanized. For instance, a slave is a dehumanized being, for he may be bought or sold (economic object-function). However, thinking about, or naming, a human being does not turn him into a logical or a lingual object, because such thinking and naming are always embedded in the social relationships that humans have among themselves, such as parents giving names to their children.

3. The fact that humans are the only beings that function as

subjects in all sixteen modal aspects has an interesting implication. Humans are logical, historical, lingual, social, etc. beings. That is, they are the only beings in our cosmic reality—as far as we know—that are subject to *norms*. If dogs are badly trained, they may become quite asocial, as we might say. But in reality, a dog cannot obey or disobey social norms. It can only behave in a way that we, in our society, experience as socially undesirable, which is usually Man's fault, not the dog's fault. Strictly speaking, a dog cannot behave socially or asocially. It can only follow instinctive or acquired behavioral patterns. But Man is a social being who can behave in a social or an asocial way, thereby obeying or disobeying social norms.

4. The fact that Man can consciously disobey spiritive norms has an interesting consequence: he can feel bad about it. That is because he has a *conscience*. In this word we find the Latin word *scientia*, meaning "knowledge." Your conscience means that, when you have disobeyed a spiritive norm, you know it and regret it. You may commit logical or lingual errors, you may make social or economic mistakes; these things do not touch your conscience very much. *Errare humanum est*, "it is human to err" now and then. But sometimes you realize that you could or should have known better, or that you made a certain logical, formative, social, or economic mistake *on purpose*, to serve your own interests. In these cases a juridical or moral element comes in, and your conscience is speaking. Animals do not have a conscience. They may fear certain consequences of certain actions, because they know from experience that these unpleasant consequences usually follow upon these actions. But they cannot juridically, or morally, or pistically, judge their own actions.

Christian Meaning

Christian philosophers will recognize the matters just mentioned more easily than secular philosophers. That is the case, firstly, because the former are aware of the special nature of Man as a religious being before God. Animals are obedient to *natural laws* only. Man is also supposed to obey *norms*. This makes him a responsible (or response-able) being, that is, a being who can, or can refuse to, respond to God's call. Part of God's call is expressed in the norms that God has embedded within his creation.

Secondly, the distinction between subject and object-functions is proper to a genuinely Christian philosophy as well. This might surprise you. What is so "Christian" about subject and object-functions? Let me explain.

In a biblical view of creation it is essential that all things have been created not only for God, but also for Man. All things have been created for the glory of God, but also as a kingdom over which Adam and Eve were placed as king and queen (Gen. 1:26-28). Within cosmic reality, nothing whatsoever has been created by God that has no reference to Man. Secular philosophy would never concede such a point, but in Christian philosophy it is of vital importance. Everything was created in reference to Man, and, after the fall and redemption, everything relates to the Second Man, the Last Adam, Jesus Christ (cf. 1 Cor. 15:45, 47). In and through him, God has created all things, and in and through him, all things are going to be restored to God (Col. 1:15-22).

By recognizing the object-functions of things, we recognize not only the functioning of these things under the law of God (subject-functions), but also the way they function in the life of higher beings: lifeless things in the lives of plants, animals, and humans; plants in the lives of animals and humans; lower animals in the lives of higher animals and humans; and higher animals in the lives of humans. The recognition of object-functions is the recognition of Man as the crown of creation, and the way all things function in their relationships to Man—Adam first, and in the end, Christ.

We have found at least four things in this chapter that are characteristic of a Christian philosophy. I am not saying that no secular philosopher could ever have thought of them but, to my mind, they are far more likely to be found in a Christian philosophy:

1. The whole array of (about) sixteen modal aspects of cosmic reality (*no idolatrous absolutization of any single aspect*).

2. The recognition of the law side of cosmic reality, and the specific way it functions within the various modal aspects (this is the *recognition of God's laws for creation*).

3. Man is subject not only to natural laws, as are all creatures in cosmic reality, but also to norms. This gives him a very special position within God's creation, a position of *responsibility*. Strictly speaking, animals cannot disobey God, but Man can. He is placed highest in creation—but he can also fall the deepest. Animals cannot fall into sin, but Man can, and he did.

4. The subject- and object-functions of things, a distinction that enables us to state that *all* things within the cosmos function in *all* modal aspects (this is the *recognition of Man's central position in cosmic reality*).

I hope you are starting to like Christian philosophy!

Kernels

Let us now take another step forward by trying to formulate the essence, the kernel, of every modal aspect. That may seem to be quite easy. The essence of the arithmetical aspect is *number*, that of the spatial aspect is *extended form*, that of the kinematic aspect is *motion*, that of the energetic aspect is *force*, that of the biotic aspect is *life,* etc. However, a great danger is looming here because each of these terms may refer to something "thing-like." I told you before how easily the "thing side" of reality is confused with its "aspect side." It is true to say that numbers, spatiality, motions, forces and lives have no independent being; in this sense, they are not things. But they do have a "thing-like" character in the sense that we can speak of this or that number (or form, motion, force, life). And this or that number (or spatial form, motion, force, life) can never be the kernel of a *modal aspect*.

It is quite difficult to formulate the essence of a modal aspect in such a way as to avoid the smallest possibility of confusing it with something "thing-like." Things move; they undergo motion. This pertains to the "thing side" of reality. On the "aspect side" of reality we might say something like this: reality has a motion aspect in that all things can move, or be moved. Just as it has a numerical aspect in that things can be counted, it has a force aspect, a life aspect, etc.

As far as I am concerned, I prefer to stick to the adjectives mentioned: there is a spatial, a logical, an economic aspect to reality, etc., without using misleading nouns. At best, I might illustrate the essence of these aspects by adding something like this: the sensitive aspect has to do with the feeling side of reality, the lingual aspect has to do with the symbolic signification side, the economic aspect with the value and equilibrium side, the aesthetic aspect with the harmony and beauty side, the juridical aspect with the justice side, the ethical aspect with the love side, and the pistical aspect with the belief or confidence side of cosmic reality.

Let me clarify this point by using some simple illustrations. Things have a certain beauty (or ugliness, for that matter); that is, they function in the aesthetic aspect, or they have an aesthetic function. Human acts may have a loving—or not so loving—character; that is, they function in the ethical aspect, or they have an ethical function. States of affairs always have a legal aspect; that is, they function in the juridical aspect, or they have a juridical function. But always keep things and modal aspects apart. They are like two different dimensions of reality, perpendicular to one another. You can place them in a square with "things" on the horizontal axis, and "aspects" on the vertical axis. If you have, say, twelve different "things" in the horizontal axis (the number is arbitrary), plotted against our sixteen "aspects," you get twelve times sixteen equals one hundred ninety-two little squares, each with its own specific meaning. But never confuse the horizontal axis and the vertical axis!

I recommend that you play with these ideas—things and aspects—yourself, until you can say that you have really mastered this complicated distinction between the "thing side" and the "aspect side" of cosmic reality. I can tell you that even experienced Christian philosophers still confuse them from time to time!

Analogies

I am now going to make things even more complicated. I never claimed that Christian philosophy, or philosophy in general, is a simple thing!

Consider, for example, a term like *strength*. Of what modal aspect would you think right away when you hear this term? The energetic aspect, I would suppose. *Strength* is a typically energetic term, so you would think. But wait a second. We also speak of "strong" feelings, a "strong" argument, a "strong" historical development, a "strong" saying, a "strong" bond between certain people, a "strong" market, a "strong" sense of beauty (or, of justice, of morality), and a "strong" faith. In none of these cases are we dealing with a strength or energy that can be expressed in newtons or joules. On the contrary, these are sensitive, logical, historical, lingual, social, economic, aesthetic, juridical, ethical and pistical examples of strength, respectively.

We find that there is *force* that can be expressed in newtons, and there is *force* that cannot. What kind of phenomenon are we facing here? Some may argue that, in the latter cases, it is a matter of metaphors. But that is too simple. To some extent, metaphors always have an arbitrary character. If we speak of a "broken heart," or say, "It's raining cats and dogs," we use metaphors. It is characteristic of metaphors that they can be easily replaced by other expressions. But when we speak of "strong" feelings, a "strong" market, or a "strong" faith, we discover that it is virtually impossible to replace the word "strong" here by another word that is not a synonym. It seems that "strength" is indeed a term that in some way or another finds a place in every modal aspect. In the energetic aspect, we encounter "strength" in its original sense (rule of thumb: this is always strength/energy that can be measured in newtons or joules). In the other aspects, we encounter "strength" in what we call an *analogical* sense.

Analogies play an important role in the theory of modal aspects, but also in all the special sciences. It turns out that all modal aspects are intertwined, because within each aspect we find analogies with all the other aspects. If there are sixteen aspects, this means there are, in principle, fifteen analogies within each aspect; when we multiply sixteen aspects times fifteen analogies, we get a total of two hundred forty analogies!

Look at the examples mentioned: with the notion of strong feelings we are dealing with an energetic analogy within the sensitive aspect. Strong feelings are primarily a sensitive matter, but with reference to the energetic modality. With a strong argument, or in terms of a forceful argument, we find an energetic analogy within the logical aspect. In a strong historical development we find an energetic analogy within the historical aspect. In a strong saying we find an energetic analogy within the lingual aspect. In a strong bond between certain people we find an energetic analogy within the social aspect. In a strong market we find an energetic analogy within the economic aspect. With a strong faith we find an energetic analogy within the pistical aspect.

In all these cases, determine first what is the characteristic aspect of the matter, and then find the aspect to which a reference is being made. In this way, you may find interesting pairs: in a strong market we find an energetic analogy within the economic aspect, but in a balanced division of force within a machine we have the opposite: an economic analogy within the energetic aspect.

Let us also take some examples from one single modality, say, the logical one. In multiplied thoughts we have to do with an arithmetical analogy within the logical modality, and so on: thinking space (spatial); "his thoughts moved this way" (kinematic); "I feel this is right" (sensitive); "life of thinking" (German: *Denkleben*; Dutch: *denkleven*; biotic); balanced thinking (economic); beautiful thoughts (aesthetic); faith thinking (German: *Glaubensdenken*; Dutch: *geloofsdenken*; pistical).

Try to work out some other examples for yourself!

The Law as Boundary

In Christian philosophy, we sometimes speak of the law as the boundary between God and the cosmos. God is on one side of this boundary, that is, he is above the law, whereas the cosmos is on the other side of this boundary, that is, all created reality is under the law. God is the Lawgiver, the cosmos is that to which the law has been given. Nothing that is divine is under the law, and nothing that has been created is above the law. Please note: as a man, Jesus is under the law-order, but as the Son, in and through whom God created all things, he is above the law-order.

In this terminology, the term *boundary* is not to be taken in a spatial sense as if you could supply coordinates for this boundary. As such, the term *boundary* is a spatial term, but we use it here only as a metaphor. We may ask, though, whether it is a very appropriate metaphor. It might suggest a dividing line between God and his creation, and that is certainly not my intention. This boundary not only separates but also connects. The law could also be called the *connection point* between God and his cosmos.

It is not so easy to find appropriate metaphors here. Dooyeweerd himself complicates the matter by also speaking of the law as a "side" of cosmic reality: the "law-side" is distinct from the "subject-side" or "factual side" of it (recall the beginning of this chapter). In this terminology, the fact that *laws* and *things* belong inseparably together is more adequately expressed. These are two "sides" of the same creation that are as inseparable as the two sides of a coin: things are under laws, and laws are valid for things.

Interestingly we may conclude that in speaking of the law as boundary, we are emphasizing the *uncreated* aspect of the law: it is God's own Word *for* creation. His Word is not created but spoken; it is the Word of his own mouth. However, when speaking of the law as "side," we are underscoring the *created* aspect of the law: the law side is a "side" of creation as such.

Laws in this sense are not like the Sinaitic law, "a yoke that neither we nor our ancestors have been able to bear" (Acts 15:10). Laws have not been given to make the existence of things miserable, but to make them at all *possible*. All things (including living things) have a certain structure, which functions as a kind of law for them (see chapter 5). It goes somewhat like this: "If you want to be an elephant, you need to be a huge mammal with a thick skin and a big, very versatile trunk." Laws are ways to describe how things function. Dogs bark, otherwise they are not dogs. That is a way to describe a function. You can turn this into a law: "If you want to be a dog, one of the conditions is that you bark." Barking identifies you as a dog. There are no things without laws that define and condition their structure, without laws that make them what they are. There are no things without laws, just as there are no laws without things that obey them.

So you see the terms "law-side" and "subject-side" are quite helpful. But in fact, the term *boundary* is also useful. It helps us to distinguish between what is above and under this boundary. If you do not make this distinction, you may run into all kinds of trouble. For instance, by obliterating this boundary between God and his creation you end up in pantheism (God and the cosmos are identical). That is one error you might commit. Other philosophers have made the mistake of lifting certain elements of creation above the boundary as if they were divine, by suggesting, for instance—as Scholastic philosophers did—that human reason is not affected by sin. Over against this, Christian philosophy maintains that *all* cosmic reality was affected by sin through the fall of Man, and that to exempt parts of it amounts to deifying these parts. Everything above the boundary is sinless, everything under the boundary is affected by sin. (Jesus as a man was not affected by sin, but he shared our flesh that, in us, was sinful flesh; cf. Heb. 2:14; Rom. 8:3).

Other thinkers have made the opposite mistake by trying to pull God below the boundary. For instance, if you claim that God sometimes acts, or seems to act, in an arbitrary way, you place him under the law. To understand this, consider the fact that only if a being is under the law can you establish whether his conduct is lawful, or whether it is arbitrary. Certain actions by God could be considered to be arbitrary only if other actions by him could be considered to be lawful. But that is impossible because God is above the law.

The great Reformer, John Calvin, made this famous statement about God: *Deus legibus solutus est, sed non exlex*, "God is free from (or above) laws, but not law-*less*"; that is, he never acts in an arbitrary way. He is always faithful to himself; he "cannot disown [or deny, or be false to] himself" (cf. 2 Tim. 2:13). This point could be expressed this way: God is a law unto himself in the sense that he could never act against his own nature. But he is never under the laws that he himself instituted for his creation.

Structure and Direction

Christian philosophy makes an important distinction between *structure* and *direction* (Vollenhoven). The term *structure* has to do with the creational structures, the structural laws that God has instituted for the various creatures and cosmic modalities. *Direction* is a dimension that is, so to speak, perpendicular to that of structure; it involves the directedness of any entity, event, or state of affairs. There are numerous structures, but there are only two directions: either the positive direction toward the Creator and his honor, or the apostate direction, away from the Creator, to his dishonor.

With the help of these two dimensions, we can now explain how the fall of Man has changed the *direction* of the human heart. Man's natural, i.e. unredeemed, heart is no longer directed towards God and his honor, but apostatically (a word related to *apostasy*) directed away from the Creator toward the false gods. However, the fall did not change the *structural* dimension of cosmic reality because that would mean that the law-order was changed. How could sin change God's own powerful, permanent creational Word? Sin did not alter God's ordinances but the functioning of creatures under these ordinances. If sin had disturbed the law-order as well, this would imply that Man's fall had destroyed the very nature of creation. That would mean that sin and Satan play an autonomous role over against God, a claim that would affect God's very sovereignty. The law has not changed, but Man's functioning under the law has changed.

Also after the fall, the laws to which reality is subject may still be called creational ordinances. They are still the original laws as God has instituted them for creation. In the manner in which God has maintained the cosmic law-order, also after the fall, his grace and covenantal faithfulness toward fallen humanity come to light. By this faithfulness, he causes the sun to rise on the evil and the good, and sends rain on the righteous and the unrighteous (Matt. 4:45). By this grace, nature and human society after the fall have not been delivered up to the power of evil. As a consequence, they have not fallen apart but remained intact. This grace has been referred to as God's "common grace," to be distinguished from "special grace," which comes to light in redemption.

In summary, the structures have not been changed, but the direction of the human heart, which has turned away from God and his law. Natural Man may still speak in a linguistically correct way, but his language is basically idolatrous. He still forms proper societal relationships, but the essential religious direction of them is turned away from God. Natural Man still does science, often in a superb way, but his science too is principally directed to false gods. Natural Man and regenerated Man still stand under the same divine law-order, but they live out of different directional heart choices. In the thinking, speaking, and acting of both groups, the norms and principles of God's law are presupposed. But whereas the God-directed person has chosen obedience to these norms as his life's basis—though in practice he may fail in this—the idol-directed person lives parasitically off God's law in disobedience. Natural Man is a parasite because, through God's "common grace," God's law sustains his life as well, whereas he attempts to live as if only his own laws hold for him. Sin always presupposes God's law since disobedience to God implicitly refers to divine laws that are not being obeyed. Thus, the harm of, say, lying and stealing, implicitly refers to the norms "You shall not lie," or "You shall not steal."

Sin and Redemption

Because Man is the head and steward of creation, sin has an effect on all *culture*, a term referring to all human action through which the potentialities of creation are unfolded. However, sin also has an effect on natural phenomena. It was not the natural laws that were changed, but human action in nature. We see this in the way Man either actively spoils nature—exploitation, pollution, mismanagement, destruction—or passively experiences failure in managing nature and controlling natural phenomena. Actually, this is Man's *cultural mandate* we are speaking about (see chapter 5): as a steward he fails miserably in the task he has in regard to nature. However, for the strictly scientific study of nature, this fact makes no difference. The reason is that natural science is aimed at the unveiling of the cosmic order of the natural laws, and these were not changed through Man's fall.

As I said, in and through Christ, the Son of God, all things were created; in and through Christ, the Son of Man, all things are redeemed and restored to God. If the law-order was not changed through the fall, there is no need for any redemption of the law-order. That which is redeemed is Man under the law-order, and creation that under the influence of Man came under the power of sin. Therefore, this new creation is not a world governed by a new divine law-order. No, it is a world in which the apostate direction of the human heart and the subsequent corruption of the world is bent back toward God. This takes place on the basis of Christ's work of atonement, out of repentant Man's faith, and by the Holy Spirit. Because of this bending back toward God, we can speak of God-directed people, who have chosen the obedience to God's law to be their principle of life. We speak of *principle* because the realization of this obedience in practice is often still sinful.

Such God-directed (redeemed, believing) people are those who take the appeal of God's Word seriously again and work this out in a practical way. To them, this means being followers (disciples) of Christ, citizen-subjects in his kingdom (cf. Matt. 28:18-20; Rom. 14:17-18; Col. 1:13), through the power of the Holy Spirit (cf. 1 Cor. 4:20). Already now, before the second coming of Christ, this implies the manifestation and dissemination of the kingdom of God throughout the world.

As I said, science is oriented toward a law-order that was not affected by sin. But the way science is done has definitely been affected by sin, just like all human activity. Therefore, Man's redemption also involves a cleansing of the way he deals with nature and culture, and the way he investigates them scientifically. However, here too, the working of sin still remains present. Only at the end of history will the power of sin be definitively broken and destroyed (cf. John 1:29). Only then will all things perfectly answer to the appeal of God's law. Even science will be redeemed!

Questions for Review

1. Explain the difference between the "ordered world" and the "world order."

2. What is an important difference between the laws of the lower law-spheres (the natural ones), and those of the higher law-spheres (the spiritive ones)?

3. Give some illustrations of the difference between natural laws and spiritive norms.

4. Why is it important to distinguish between what natural laws and spiritive norms are, on the one hand, and our knowledge of them, on the other hand?

5. Explain and illustrate subject-functions and object-functions.

6. What does it mean to say: "All things function in all modal aspects, either as subjects or as objects"?

7. Why do human beings have no object-functions? What does it mean that only human beings function as subjects in all sixteen modal aspects?

8. List some important philosophical points in which Christian philosophy differs from other philosophies.

9. Explain how we get a total of two hundred forty analogies or analogical senses for describing cosmic reality.

10. In what sense has the term boundary been used in this chapter, and why could it be called necessary and helpful for a Christian philosophy?

11. What are the meaning and importance of the terms structure and direction as described in this chapter?

12. Why are the ideas of structure and direction important for understanding, for instance, sin and redemption? Why are these ideas important for doing science?

Chapter Five

A CHRISTIAN VIEW
OF ENTITIES

In the previous chapters, I have tried to give you some idea of the "aspect-side" of cosmic reality. We have distinguished sixteen modal aspects, and have looked at the fascinating theory that *all* things in cosmic reality function in *all* sixteen aspects. This is the case if you allow not only for subject-functions, but also for object-functions.

Now the time has come for us to turn from the "aspect-side" to the "thing-side" of reality. It may sound stupid, but the question I want to lay before you is: What are things? In philosophy you have to get used to questions that may sound stupid or self-evident. That is because philosophers do not want to take anything for granted. In their view, nothing is self-evident. That is why they always ask: What is this? and Why is this? and How is this? and What is this for?

If you have no feel for this kind of questions, no problem. You undoubtedly have other gifts. But philosophers, or those who have the gifts of becoming a philosopher, *love* these questions. They possess the uncommon gift of *wondering*. "Stop and consider God's wonders" (Job 37:14b). Already the great Greek philosopher Plato (429-347 B.C.) said that all philosophy starts with this capacity to wonder, to be amazed about things, events, and states of affairs that appear to other people as self-evident. This is the ability to take nothing for granted but to always ask questions that other people do not recognize as valid and meaningful problems.

So you may think you already *know* what a thing is, but think about it. How would you *define* a thing? I mean "thing" in the broadest sense of the term, including plants, animals, and humans. It is strange to call a human a "thing," so let's use a more philosophical term: *entity*. This word comes from the Latin *ens*, which means "being." An entity is something that "is," something that exists within our empirical reality.

In order to define things, we must first define *defining*. (You see again, nothing is self-evident!) Ever since Plato's pupil, that other great Greek philosopher, Aristotle (384-322 B.C.), we do this first by referring to a higher category (Latin: *genus proximum*), and then by pointing out in what respects this thing differs from other things within this category (Latin: *differentia specifica*). For instance, elephants are mammals with a highly versatile proboscis. The *genus proximum* here is mammals, and the specific difference (or the point in which elephants differ from all other mammals) is "having a highly versatile proboscis" (not just "having a proboscis," since aardvarks and tapirs have a proboscis, too).

If this is what *defining* means, can we define entities in the same way? Let's try. Entities are empirical creatures, that is, creatures within our empirical reality. The *genus proximum* is creatures (things and beings created by God), and the specific difference is empirical (things and beings that can be observed by humans). This excludes angels because they do not belong to our empirical reality (leaving aside the point that some people *have* seen angels—but these were in fact *appearances* of angels who were entering temporarily into our empirical world).

Let me immediately add a point here that should not be overlooked. You have to distinguish between entities and properties of entities. An emotion is not an entity—it is a state in which certain entities, namely, higher animals and humans, may be living at a given moment. The rule of thumb is that a genuine entity always functions in all sixteen aspects of cosmic reality, whereas, for instance, an emotion does not. It is connected with one function only, namely, the sensitive function. Emotion is not a thing, but refers to the sensitive aspect of things (see the previous chapter).

Kinds of Entities

In order to come up with a useful classification of entities, we make use of the very helpful theory of the modal aspects. Let's begin by distinguishing between five categories or classes:

1. *Inanimate things*, such as brooks and stones, have subject-

functions in the first four modalities (arithmetical, spatial, kinematic, and energetic), and object-functions in all the higher modalities, from the biotic to the pistical modality. The most *characteristic* modality, that is, the one that best describes the nature of inanimate things, is their highest subject-function: the energetic modality. We could say that inanimate things are energetically qualified—in brief, energetic—entities, without forgetting for a moment that they *always* function in *all* modalities.

2. *Plants* have subject functions in the first *five* modalities (arithmetical, spatial, kinematic, energetic, and biotic), and have object-functions in all the higher modalities. The most *characteristic* modality, that is, the one that best describes the nature of plants, is their highest subject-function: the biotic modality. We could say that plants are biotically qualified—in short, biotic—entities, and again we remember that plants function in all modalities; the biotic aspect is just the qualifying one. (As always in this book, "qualifying" means, "expressing its quality," i.e., its being thus-and-so.)

3. *Lower animals* have subject-functions in the first six modalities (arithmetical, spatial, kinematic, energetic, biotic, and perceptive), and have object-functions in all the higher modalities. The most *characteristic* modality, that is, the one that best describes the nature of lower animals, is their highest subject-function: the perceptive modality. We could say that lower animals are perceptive entities, that is, entities that can perceive, but that have no true affections and emotions.

4. *Higher animals* have subject-functions in the first *seven* modalities (arithmetical, spatial, kinematic, energetic, biotic, perceptive, and sensitive), and object-functions in all the higher modalities, from the logical to the pistical. The most *characteristic* modality, that is, the one that best describes the nature of higher animals, is their highest subject-function: the sensitive modality. We could say that higher animals are sensitive entities, that is, entities that not only can perceive, but also have true affections and emotions.

5. *Humans* have subject-functions in *all sixteen* modalities, and no object-functions. Interestingly, in this case, the most *characteristic* modality, that is, the one that best describes the nature of

humans, is not their highest subject-function: the pistical modality (as Vollenhoven originally claimed; later he changed his mind). That is the case, first, because Man's mental activities can be qualified by any of the spiritive modalities, and secondly, because humans are in the unique position of being more than just the sum of their sixteen subject-functions. We will come back to this essential point in the next chapter, where we will present a brief introduction to Christian philosophical anthropology.

Of course, this division into five categories can be refined much further. There are numerous kinds of inanimate things, numerous species and genuses (or genera) among plants and animals, and several races among humans. But this is a matter to be studied by the special sciences, so we will not investigate this subject in this book.

By now, you may have come to understand that, as Christian philosophers, we are particularly interested in the object-functions of inanimate things and living beings. The reason is that, as I explained before, these object-functions tell us a lot about the relationships that inanimate things and living beings have with Man as the crown of creation.

Nature and Culture

This is a good place to introduce another, well-known distinction briefly mentioned before: the distinction between nature and culture. Let us put it this way: on the one hand, *nature* is the whole of those parts of cosmic reality that are unspoiled and pristine, i.e., unaffected by Man. On the other hand, *culture* is the whole of those parts of cosmic reality that *have* been affected by Man in a positive sense. *Culture is manipulated (handled, shaped) nature; it is nature as worked or processed by Man.*

Christians believe that Man has received a divine *command* to work nature: "The LORD God took the man and put him in the Garden of Eden to work it and take care of it" (Gen. 2:15; cf. 3:23, "So the LORD God banished him from the Garden of Eden to work the ground from which he had been taken."). This activity may be taken to mean working nature in the broadest sense. In this context, Christian theologians and philosophers, beginning with Abraham Kuyper (see chapter 3), often speak of the *cultural mandate* God gave to Man: the command to work (shape) nature. The result is culture, varying from agriculture (note the word "culture" in this—"culture" in its original meaning) and building houses (architecture), roads, and bridges, to industrial processing in homes (home crafts), laboratories or factories (technology), and the arts (music, visual arts, literature, etc.). Culture may even include Man himself; obvious examples are education (shaping young persons), physical and mental training, bodybuilding and body culture, and the like.

In Christian philosophy, we describe culture as the specific way in which the *object-functions* of non-human entities have been opened up by Man (leaving aside education and training of humans, for the time being). Entities have enormous potentialities, which are developed by humans. The horse was already present within the marble, so to speak, before Michelangelo brought it out; in our terms, he *activated* the aesthetical object-function of the marble in a splendid way. The wooden house was already present in the timber before the builder "unveiled" it; in our terms, he *activated* the formative object-function of the wood in an expert way. The highly cultivated rose was genetically already present in the original wild rose; in our terms, the gardener activated the social and aesthetic object-functions of the original rose in a clever way.

You can easily see that it is highly inadequate to describe Michelangelo's horse as an "energetic thing" (the energetic modality being the highest subject-function of the marble). Likewise, it is highly inadequate to describe the builder's wooden house or the gardener's cultivated rose as a "biotic thing" (the biotic modality being the highest subject-function of the timber or the rose). No, the marble horse is primarily an aesthetic thing, the wooden house is primarily a *social* thing, and the cultivated rose is at least both social and aesthetic.

Here we encounter an interesting state of affairs. With regard to cultural products, it is never the highest *subject*-functions that describe their true nature, but certain *object*-functions. The aesthetic realm, to which Michelangelo's horse and the grower's rose belong, encompasses aesthetic subjects—these are always humans, like Michelangelo and the gardener, both artists and art experts—as well as their aesthetic objects: works of art, created by artists, or works (beautiful plants and animals) by expert growers, as well as critical reviews by art experts.

Here is another example. The social realm comprises social subjects—again always humans, in this case acting as social beings—as well as their social objects: cultural products that are essential to human social life in the broadest sense, including houses, streets, public buildings, modes of transport, telecommunication systems, mobile phones, etc.

As you will understand, we can speak similarly about the *logical* realm (humans plus logical objects such as university buildings and scientific handbooks), the *formative* realm (humans plus formative objects such as historical achievements or technical products), the *lingual* realm (humans plus lingual objects such as dictionaries, but also traffic signs, logos, etc.), the *economic* realm (humans plus economic objects such as banks, securities, coins, banknotes), the *juridical* realm (humans plus juridical objects such as legal aid centers, tribunals, and prisons), the *ethical* realm (humans plus ethical objects such as engagement rings and birthday gifts), and the *pistical* realm (humans plus pistical objects such as church buildings, pulpits, baptismal fonts, synagogues, mosques, temples, altars).

The Notion of the Idionomy

In order to understand the nature of entities, the theory as we have investigated it so far is not yet sufficient. We have to take another step forward. At the end of the previous chapter, I explained that laws have been given to make the existence of things *possible*. All entities, including living organisms, have a certain structure, which functions as a kind of law for them. You can say that Thing P has structure thus-and-so. You can also say that if you want to be thing P, you have to have structure thus-and-so. That is, the structure of a thing is at the same time a law for this thing. As I said before, there are no empirical things without laws that define and condition or qualify their structure, laws that make them what they are.

In this connection, Dooyeweerd spoke of the "individuality

structures" of entities. Others have suggested terms like "identity structure" or "idionomy" (Piet Verburg). The Greek word *idios* means "proper to," and *nomos* means "law." An *idionomy* is the law that is proper to a certain entity (or more precisely, a *class* of entities), the law that makes the entity the entity that it is, that describes its structure. I like the term *idionomy* because it is nice and short. "Individuality" may be misleading here because the reference is not to specific individual entities but to classes of entities. The individuality structure (idionomy) of horses refers to *all* horses, not to your specific horse. That is, the idionomy is a kind of law that makes all horses, not just your horse, to be horses: "if you want to be a horse, you have to fulfill conditions A, B, and C."

The idionomy of a certain entity is characterized by certain specific modal aspects. Firstly, inanimate things, along with plants and animals, always have what is called a *foundational* function. According to a later view of Dooyeweerd, in tangible things (inanimate things, plants, animals), this foundational function is the spatial function: each of these things is a *res extensa*, an "extended" thing, that is, a thing that takes up space (cf. Descartes).

Secondly, in Dooyeweerd's terminology, each thing also has a *qualifying* function, which indicates its "quality" (its being thus-and-so, its true nature). This is always the highest *subject*-function. In your car, this qualifying function is the energetic function. In your ornamental plant, this is the biotic function. In both your champion milk cow and your lapdog, this is the sensitive function.

Thirdly, in the use that Man makes of them, such entities also have what is called the *destination* function; this indicates the destination (purpose) of an entity within human life. With your car, this is the social function (because cars, just like pedestrians and cyclists, take part in street traffic). For your ornamental plant, this is the aesthetic function. With your champion milk cow, this is the economic function. With your lapdog, this is the ethical function (because the characteristic of a lapdog is that it is cherished by its owner). So with most things—because Man can use all things—the idionomy is characterized by at least two modal functions: the foundational function and the destination function. With cars, these are the energetic and the social functions, respectively; with ornamental plants the biotic and the aesthetic functions; with champion milk cows the sensitive and the economic functions; and with lapdogs the sensitive and the ethical functions.

When natural things (inanimate things, plants, animals) are culturally manipulated (worked, processed), we get cultural products. In such products, there is even a fourth modal function that stands out. This function may be called the *typical* function. (The actual names are not so important as long as you are consistent in the way you use them.) In cultural entities, this is always the formative function: inanimate things, along with plants and animals, can be formed (shaped, manipulated, processed; animals can also be educated, trained) for a certain purpose.

Please note that, in the end, idionomies cannot be conceptually grasped. We use the theory of modal aspects to approximate the matter, to get an idea of what idionomies are all about. To a certain extent, you can even define them: a car is a motorized, four-wheeled mode of transport that has seats for no more than six persons. A dog is a barking carnivore. But do you now know what a *car* or a *dog* is? At best, you can form an idea of them, even a rational idea because you can argue about it. At the same time, your idea of them transcends the totality of modal aspects, as do all matters of which we can only form an idea. Think of the kernels of the various modal aspects. These cannot even be defined, because there is no *genus proximum* to which we might refer. We can only form an idea of them.

Encapsis

We will keep moving forward, and will now take another big step. Consider the car again. It consists mostly of steel, an alloy of iron and carbon, plus perhaps some wood, some textile or leather, and some synthetic materials. There is no doubt about it that this steel has its own idionomy. As such, it functions in all sixteen modal aspects of cosmic reality, irrespective of the question of what thing has been made out of this steel. Both the steel and the car have their own idionomies! There is one single car, but it seems we must assume that it possesses at least two different idionomies.

Moreover, these two idionomies are intertwined in a specific way, which Dooyeweerd had described with the term *encapsis*.

This term may remind you of the word *encapsulate*. It means that a certain matter may be encapsulated within some other matter. In a parallel way, we could say that the idionomy of the steel is encapsulated within the idionomy of the car. In other words, there is an encaptic intertwinement of the two idionomies.

Actually, in Christian philosophy we use the word *encapsis* for many different forms of such intertwinement. For instance, we use the term for *symbiotic encapsis* as in the case of the yucca plant and the yucca moth. Or we use it for *correlative encapsis* as between a living being and its habitat, or between a church and a state. Or we speak of a *subject-object encapsis,* as in the case of the snail and its shell, or the spider and its web.

It is quite important to understand this notion of encapsis in a correct way. For instance, there is an encaptic relationship between a snail and its shell, but this does not mean that the shell is a "part" of the snail. Here is a rule of thumb: the two have very different idionomies! The shell is energetically qualified, but the snail is perceptively qualified. This is an important point that you have to note very carefully. Consider a living cell, which always has clear parts, such as the nucleus and the mitochondria; they are parts of the cell because they derive their (biotically qualified) idionomy from the cell as a whole. But the molecules within that cell are *not* parts of it, for they have an (energetically qualified) idionomy of their own. Their energetic idionomy is encapsulated within, or encaptically intertwined with, the biotic idionomy of the cell.

Actually, to my mind, of all the types of encapsis, this is the most interesting one. We refer to it as *foundational encapsis.* That is, one idionomy forms a foundation for another idionomy; together they form an *encaptic whole.* The idionomy of the molecules within the cell forms the foundation for the idionomy of the cell as such. Without this idionomy—without molecules—there could be no cell. At the same time, the cell is much more than the sum total of its molecules. It has an idionomy of its own, that is qualified by the biotic aspect, whereas the idionomy of the molecules is qualified by the energetic aspect.

It is the same with the example of the car mentioned above; the difference is that this is not a natural example, like the cell, but a cultural example: the car is a man-made product. The idionomy of the steel is foundationally encapsulated within the idionomy of the car; again, together they form an *encaptic whole*. Without the steel, there is no car. But the car is much more than an amount of steel (and some other products). The organization of a car, its structure, cannot be derived from the structure of the steel; it is something of its own. The structure of the car is superimposed upon the structure of the steel, like the structure of a cathedral is superimposed upon the structure of the bricks. The idionomies are intertwined, but remain distinct.

It is very different in the cases of the ornamental plant, the champion milk cow, or the lapdog, because they do not involve some kind of foundational encapsis but rather some form of correlative encapsis with their environment. There is no *encaptic whole* involved.

Please note that, like the molecules in the living cell, the steel and the other building materials are not parts of the car. Parts of the automobile are the engine, the seats, the steering wheel, etc., which all derive their idionomy from the idionomy of the car as a whole. But the steel is not a part, because it has its own idionomy— an idionomy that, as I said, is foundationally encapsulated within the idionomy of the car. The idionomy of the steel is energetically qualified, and the idionomy of the car is socially qualified. This fact is, in itself, already sufficient to prove that the steel is not part of the car because it has its own idionomy. (Please, keep in mind that all these idionomies always function in *all* modal aspects of cosmic reality!)

The Structure of a Plant

Let us now investigate in what way the notions of idionomy and encapsis can help us to get an idea of some of the most interesting entities in our cosmic reality. We will limit ourselves to the animate world, and will start with plants. Parallel to what I said about the living cell, we can easily acknowledge that in a plant we are dealing with (at least) two idionomies. The first one is the *energetic* idionomy. Like all idionomies, this idionomy functions in all sixteen modal aspects of cosmic reality, but it is *qualified* by the energetic aspect. It consists of the whole molecular structure of the plant. Remember, this is a lifeless structure! This energetic idionomy is foundationally encapsulated within the second idionomy, which makes the plant a living entity. This idionomy, too, functions in all sixteen modal aspects of cosmic reality, but it is *qualified* by the biotic aspect.

Please note the difference between inanimate and living here. The plant's molecular structure is inanimate, but the second, biotic idionomy makes the plant a living organism. The first, energetic, inanimate idionomy is obviously designed to "carry" (form a vehicle for) biotic (physiological) processes. Such physics as you find in the energetic idionomy of a plant you find nowhere in the inanimate cosmos. In philosophical language, the energetic idionomy of a plant has a highly activated biotic object-function. Without this idionomy there are, and there could be, no life processes in the plant. This is inanimate matter that is uniquely designed so as to condition and enable life.

This state of affairs is beautifully expressed in the term *biomolecules*. These are molecules such as proteins, nucleic acids (DNA, RNA), polysaccharides, certain lipids, etc. These molecules are produced by living organisms, but are themselves not living. The prefix "bio-" in the term "biomolecule" indicates that, although such a biomolecule in itself is inanimate, it is meant for living structures. It conditions and enables life, without being alive itself. Biomolecules, although inanimate, have no other purpose than to serve life. Life is not possible without biomolecules and, conversely, biomolecules make no sense other than in living organisms.

In this model, there is not the slightest need to reduce the biotic to the energetic, as so many philosophers (physicalists, materialists) have attempted. On the contrary, both idionomies are maintained in their own specific—biotic and energetic—character.

The first, energetic idionomy has subject-functions in the first *four* modal aspects, and has an important *internal* object-function in the biotic aspect. Here, *internal* means within the boundaries of the *encaptic whole*. For the rest, this idionomy has only external object-functions.

The second, biotic idionomy has subject-functions in the first *five* modal aspects, among which the biotic subject-function has to be mentioned in particular. Besides this, both idionomies have object-functions in the higher modalities. The object-functions of the second, biotic idionomy are of an entirely *external* nature. That is, they do not refer to what happens between the boundaries of the *encaptic whole*, but only to the lives of animals and humans in which the plant functions as an object.

The Structure of a Lower Animal

By the phrase *lower animals* I mean all invertebrates as well as possibly those (cold-blooded) vertebrates that do not possess a true life of affections and emotions. In such an animal we are dealing with (at least) three idionomies. The first one is, again, the *energetic* idionomy. Like all idionomies, it functions in all sixteen modal aspects of cosmic reality, but it is *qualified*—its quality is expressed—by the energetic aspect. It consists of the whole (inanimate!) molecular structure of the animal. This energetic idionomy is foundationally encapsulated within the second idionomy, which makes the animal a living entity. This idionomy, too, functions in all sixteen modal aspects of cosmic reality, but it is *qualified* by the biotic aspect.

This second, biotic idionomy is foundationally encapsulated within the third idionomy, which makes the animal a perceptive entity. This idionomy, too, functions in all sixteen modal aspects of cosmic reality, but it is *qualified*—its quality is expressed—by the perceptive aspect. The animal is not only a biotic organism, like the plant, but a perceptive organism as well.

Please note the difference between non-perceptive and perceptive here. The animal's biotic (physiological) structure is alive but perception-less, but the third, perceptive idionomy makes of the animal an organism that can perceive and observe. This means, for instance, that the animal exhibits stimulus-response patterns. Plants such as the Venus flytrap can respond to stimuli in that their leaves function as "snap traps": when touched by an insect the trap rapidly closes. But this is a purely mechanical process, like depositing a coin and getting coffee from a machine. In true stimulus-response patterns, there is some "black box"—some elementary form of consciousness—between the stimulus and the response, no matter how simple and primitive. This makes an animal an animal (if we leave aside unicellular organisms, in order to avoid making things too complicated).

In this case, the first, energetic idionomy is obviously designed to "carry" not only biotic (physiological) but also perceptive processes within the animal. A special kind of physics is needed, namely, physics that conditions and enables perceptive processes, such as the physical (molecular) processes in ganglia, nerve tracts and brains, no matter how primitive. These various organs themselves belong to the second, biotic idionomy of the animal. The physiology of such organs is designed so as to "carry" (condition, enable) perceptive processes. Please note, the organs as such cannot perceive—it is the *animal* that perceives. The organs have a biotic idionomy. But the physiological processes in these organs can "carry" the perceptive experiences of the animal.

Both the energetic and the biotic idionomies of the animal have highly activated *internal* perceptive object-functions, internal because they are functioning within the boundaries of the encaptic whole. Without these idionomies, there is, and there could be, no perception in animals (or humans). Plants cannot perceive; animals can. Plants do not have the appropriate physics and physiology for perception. At the same time, perception is much *more* than the physics and physiology involved. Molecules, sense organs, and brains cannot perceive—animals and humans can.

The Structure of a Higher Animal

By the phrase *higher animals* I mean all (warm-blooded) vertebrates that possess a clearly recognizable life of affections, emotions, and drives, mainly or exclusively birds and mammals. As far as I can see, in such animals we are dealing with (at least) four idionomies. The first one is, again, the *energetic* idionomy, that is, the idionomy qualified by the energetic aspect. It consists of the whole (inanimate) molecular structure of the animal. I repeat: this energetic idionomy is foundationally encapsulated within the second idionomy, which makes the animal a living entity and which is qualified by the biotic aspect. This second, biotic idionomy is foundationally encapsulated within the third idionomy, which makes the animal a perceptive entity and is qualified by the perceptive aspect.

The new point is the following. In a higher animal, this third, perceptive idionomy is foundationally encapsulated within the fourth idionomy, which makes the animal a sensitive entity and is qualified by the sensitive aspect.

Please note the difference between non-sensitive and sensitive here. The animal's perceptive structure can accommodate sensations and perceptions but is, as such, feeling-less. But the fourth, sensitive idionomy makes the animal an organism that not only can perceive and observe, but also know feelings: affections, drives, and emotions. This means, for instance, that the animal possesses certain organs that can "carry" (condition, enable) feelings, such as certain hormone-producing organs, appropriate brain parts, and an autonomous nervous system. Feelings cannot be *reduced* to the physiological processes that such organs involve. The animal's sensitive life has its own idionomy, emphatically distinct from the biotic and the perceptive idionomies.

At the same time, the latter idionomies are essential to the animal's sensitive life: no feeling without perception, no perception without physiology, no physiology without physics. Feeling is not a particular form of perception, it is not reducible to it—the sensitive modality is not reducible to the perceptive modality—but it is equally true that feeling cannot exist without, or is "carried" by, perception, just as perception cannot exist without, or, is "carried" by, biotic life. A ≠ B, but A is dependent upon B.

That is the beauty of the theory of idionomies. It makes perfectly clear how, on the hand, the sensitive life of animals (and of humans!) is rooted in its perceptive life, just as its perceptive life is rooted in its biotic life, just as its biotic life is rooted in physical processes. On the other hand, it shows how the energetic structure conditions the biotic structure, how the biotic structure conditions the perceptive structure, and how the perceptive structure conditions the sensitive structure. The idionomies are distinct but intertwined—intertwined but distinct.

This theory underscores the fact that idionomies are not reducible to each other, as well as the fascinating fact that each idionomy functions in all sixteen modalities. For a higher animal, that means four times sixteen for a total of sixty-four different functions! It would be a wonderful exercise for you if you would try to work out these sixty-four functions for yourself. This exercise will help you immensely in becoming accustomed to the concepts of foundational encapsis and encaptic wholes.

What remains is the structure of human beings. This subject is so important that our entire next chapter is devoted to it.

Questions for Review

1. What five kinds of entities are identified in this chapter?

2. How should we distinguish between nature and culture?

3. What is meant by an entity's "identity structure" or "idionomy"? How do these terms relate to the term "modal aspect"?

4. Explain the various kinds of encapsis discussed in this chapter.

5. What is meant by foundational encapsis? What is meant by correlative encapsis?

6. What idionomies pertain to plants?

7. What idionomies pertain to lower animals?

8. What idionomies pertain to higher animals?

Chapter Six

A

CHRISTIAN ANTHROPOLOGY

In the previous chapter, I tried to give an idea of how Christian philosophy approaches the structure of a plant or an animal. You could consider that as a kind of introduction to the topic we are particularly interested in: the structure of human existence.

The First Human Idionomy

At first sight, the first four human idionomies—the physical, the biotic, the perceptive, and the sensitive—seem to be identical to those of higher animals (see previous chapter). In a sense, that is true of course. But in another sense, that is a mistake. You will see that it is not difficult to explain why this is so.

The first idionomy is the *energetic* idionomy, that is, the idionomy qualified by the energetic aspect. It consists of the whole (inanimate) molecular structure of Man. But already here there is a fundamental difference from animals: *Man needs a kind of physics that can carry his spiritive life.* (Please recall that we are using the verb carry to mean "support and enable," where process A makes process B possible, and therefore is a condition and foundation for B.) Later in this chapter, I will introduce to you the highly fascinating fifth idionomy of Man's corporeal existence, which I will call the *spiritive idionomy*. It comprises the whole of Man's spiritive (i.e., logical, formative, lingual, social, economic, aesthetic, juridical, ethical, and pistical) functioning. I will emphasize that this spiritive life cannot be reduced to Man's sensitive life, just as the latter cannot be reduced to Man's perceptive life, or his biotic life, or his physical functioning. But that is only half of the story. The other half is that there is no spiritive life without sensitive, perceptive, biotic, and physical functioning. Man's mind cannot be *reduced* to the physical, but it cannot do without the physical either.

Man's physical, biotic, perceptive, and sensitive functioning conditions and enables his spiritive functioning. Man's immanent functioning within this cosmos needs a unique kind of physics that does not exist anywhere else in the cosmos. I am referring to a physics that is designed to make spiritive phenomena—actions in the mind—at all possible. To put it a bit bluntly, I cannot send up a prayer to God without all kinds of complicated physical processes in millions of body cells. I repeat: that does not mean that praying is just physics—it would be quite naïve to conclude that—but such praying cannot do without physics. This may be a hard thing to swallow for those Christians who still believe in an absolute separation between what they call "body" and "soul" (or "spirit"). They think that they pray with their spirits or minds, and that their bodies have nothing to do with it. I will come back to this matter later in this chapter.

The Next Three Human Idionomies

The energetic idionomy of Man's corporeal existence is foundationally encapsulated within the second idionomy, which makes Man a living entity and which is qualified by the biotic aspect. Of special interest in this biotic idionomy are the organs that carry (condition, enable) the higher idionomies: sense organs (seeing, hearing, smelling, tasting, etc.) that are needed for perception, certain hormone producing organs, appropriate brain parts, and an autonomous nervous system that are needed for Man's sensitive functioning, and a brain cortex that is the essential carrier of Man's spiritive functioning.

Allow me to add two notes here. First, I repeat, because I think it is so important, that Man is not a higher animal plus a spirit (or mind). No, even his physics and his physiology are different because they must be able to carry spiritive processes, which animals do not know. Secondly, all five idionomies together comprise his corporeal existence, which is much more than physics and physiology. Here I am using the term *corporeal* in a broad sense, encompassing all Man's immanent functioning within cosmic reality.

This second, biotic idionomy is foundationally encapsulated within the third idionomy, which makes Man a perceptive entity and is qualified by the perceptive aspect. Please note that Man's perception is different from that of animals. The *sensations*, like shapes, movements and colors in seeing, and tones and timbres in hearing, may be the same, but the *perceptions* are not. Perception is the result of processing sensations in the brain. A spiritive processing of sensations goes much deeper than just a sensitive processing of them. Because Man has a spiritive structure, he is able to see not just shapes, movements, and colors, but also, for example, an elephant. That is, the shapes, movements, and colors he sees are interpreted in his brain as an elephant (or whatever the object is). Because of his spiritive structure, Man can "see" beauty and ugliness (aesthetic), just and unjust actions (juridical), good and evil deeds (ethical). We could say that it is not his eyes which see beauty, but his brain. His eyes are the same as those in mammals—but his brain is very different. And even that is not entirely correct: it is *Man* who sees beauty with the help of his brain. Mammals cannot see beauty, but Man can.

The third, perceptive idionomy is foundationally encapsulated within the fourth idionomy, which makes Man a sensitive entity and is qualified by the sensitive aspect. Just like higher animals, not only can Man perceive and observe, but he also knows feelings: affections, drives, emotions. In this sense, Man seems to be not different from higher animals. But again, to think that would be a great mistake. Man's affections, drives, and emotions are different from those of higher animals in so far as *they are able to carry spiritive processes.*

Take a simple example like blushing. You know that blushing consists of a dilation of little blood vessels in your face so that your face reddens. To that extent, it is a purely biotic phenomenon. But then, why do animals (or human babies) not blush? They possess all the physics and all the physiology that is needed for it, yet they do not do it. Why is that? It is because blushing occurs in humans at moments when they are embarrassed, or ashamed, or love-struck. Animals cannot be embarrassed, or ashamed, or love-struck because they do not have a spiritive idionomy, and babies cannot because their spiritive idionomy has not yet developed. Animals can be sexually attracted but that is quite different from being love-struck. It is the ethical aspect of the spiritive idionomy in particular that is involved here. Animals are not immoral; only Man can be immoral. Rather, animals are a-moral. Man is, among many other things, an ethical being; therefore, he can blush. Equally important is the fact that humans possesses the physics and physiology that make blushing possible.

It is these highly fascinating but intricate relationships within Man's corporeal existence that Christian philosophy tries to set out in its model of the human idionomies. This model explains how, on the one hand, Man's spiritive life is rooted in his sensitive life, just as his sensitive life is rooted in his perceptive life, just as his perceptive life is rooted in his biotic life, just as his biotic life is rooted in physical processes. On the other hand, it shows how the energetic structure conditions Man's biotic structure, how the biotic structure conditions the perceptive structure, how the perceptive structure conditions the sensitive structure, and how the sensitive structure conditions the spiritive structure. This also means that, in brief, the energetic structure conditions the spiritive structure. Man needs a physics that makes spiritive processes possible.

Also remember that idionomies are not reducible to each other, as well as the fact that each idionomy functions in all sixteen modalities. For Man, that is five times sixteen, or eighty different functions! Try to get your head around *that*!

Man's Spiritive Idionomy

In addition to all the energetic, biotic, perceptive, and sensitive idionomies that Man shares with higher animals—with all the differences I have mentioned—Man possesses what I have called a spiritive idionomy. Dooyeweerd calls it the human *act-structure*, which I find a less enlightening term. I would suggest that this *spiritive* idionomy roughly corresponds with that which, in everyday life, we call the *mind*, as long as we clearly distinguish it from the *heart* (see below).

The first thing to note is that there is no such thing as a logical idionomy, a historical idionomy, a lingual idionomy, etc. A practical indication of this fact is that Man does not have body parts (organs, brain parts) that separately carry logical, or formative, or lingual activities within the mind. Everything that goes on in his mind, that is, all these spiritive activities (acts), always function in all of the nine spiritive modalities. There is no logical activity in Man's mind that has no historical, lingual, social, economic, etc. aspects at the same time. Some acts are certainly logically *qualified*, such as certain rational arguments that are worked out in the mind.

Similarly, some acts are *formatively* qualified, for instance, historic decisions (like the decision to start a war against another nation) and technological inventions (like working out in the mind the plan for a new machine).

Some acts are *lingually* qualified—for instance, thinking about the most appropriate words in which you wish to express a delicate matter.

Some acts are *socially* qualified—for instance, thinking about what guests you are going to invite to your party.

Some acts are *economically* qualified—for instance, considering in your mind the question whether you want to buy this or that, and/or whether or not you can afford it.

Some acts are *aesthetically* qualified—for instance, weighing the question of which of the paintings, sculptures, or musical compositions you like best.

Some acts are *juridically* qualified—for instance, considering whether what you plan to do is legally acceptable or not.

Some acts are *ethically* qualified—for instance, thinking about what you can do to best show your affection—or lack thereof—for a certain person.

Some acts are *pistically* qualified—for instance, thinking of the well-known abbreviation WWJD, "What would Jesus do?"—a devout, but theologically somewhat questionable question.

Remember again that no spiritive act is possible without certain molecular processes in the brain, but that such acts cannot be *reduced* to such processes. That is precisely what the theory of the human idionomies wishes to express: these idionomies are foundationally encapsulated within each other, and thus closely interrelated, but they are not reducible to each other. Every form of reductionism is excluded here.

Surely the theory of the modal aspects is helpful but insufficient for expressing the full richness of the spiritive idionomy.

Therefore, Dooyeweerd has suggested that we should distinguish between *knowing acts, imaginative acts* and *acts of the will* as a further way to distinguish between various types of what I am calling spiritive acts. All three types of acts function in all modal aspects, with special emphasis on the nine spiritive modalities. I distinguish between them as the *cognitive*, the *(imaginative-)creative* and the *conative* dimension. For instance, if a man proposes to a lady, cognitive acts have preceded this action in that he has collected as much information about her as he can find, through her or through others. Imaginative-creative acts have preceded his proposal, too: he imagines what it would be like to be married to this lady and how he will implement his proposal. Conative acts have preceded his action, as well: in his mind he has come to the decision of his will to propose to the lady.

Of course, there is much more to be said about the spiritive idionomy, but this would easily lead us into the domains of the various humanities, psychology in particular. For instance, our spiritive acts are influenced by (a) our innate character (constitutional factors); (b) everything we have learned in our lives (operative factors); (c) our mood at a certain moment; and *last but not least*, (d) our ethos, that is, the whole of our (immanent) juridical, ethical, and pistical beliefs and values—not to be confused with our (transcendent) *faith*, to which we now turn.

Man's Ego

Man is more than his corporeal existence, which refers, as I have tried to explain, to the whole of his immanent functioning within cosmic reality. In chapter 2, I explained the important difference between the terms *immanent* and *transcendent*. In contrast with plants and animals, Man is both immanent and transcendent. That is, he functions in all sixteen *immanent* modalities of cosmic reality, and his corporeal existence encompasses five *immanent* idionomies. At the same time, he transcends (surpasses, rises above) his entire immanent functioning. The reason for this is that God has created Man in such a way that he has been designed for communication with the transcendent—primarily with God himself. Man lives fully within immanent reality, in relationship with the rest of the cosmos as its head, and at the same time Man is oriented toward the transcendent, invisible world of which God is the center.

In chapter 2, I sought to describe this matter by using a term that we know from everyday usage, but that came originally from the Bible. It is the term *heart* in its metaphorical sense. I made a distinction between the heart and its functions. The heart is transcendent, and the modal functions, from the arithmetical to the pistical, are immanent. I called the heart the "focal point" of the functions, and I called the functions the "ramifications" of the heart. These are metaphors that can help clarify matters, but that can also be replaced by other metaphors.

It is difficult to explain these matters because we all, usually without knowing it, have imbibed Greek thinking on this point. Especially in the Middle Ages, this Greek thinking was adopted in what we call *Scholastic* thinking, which was in fact the main medieval philosophy and theology. After the Reformation, Protestants took over Greek-Scholastic anthropology as well. The consequence is that Christians today walk around with Greek dualism in their minds. What does that mean?

Dichotomy and Trichotomy

A *dualism* is a view in which reality, or a part of it, is explained from two different factors (elements, dimensions, or whatever you call it) that are not only distinct from, but opposite to, each other. In anthropology, this means that Christians have become accustomed to a body-soul dualism. Man supposedly consists of two substances—as medieval thinkers would put it—namely, body and soul (or spirit). We call this a *dichotomy*, which literally means that Man is cut up into two parts: body and soul. Every time the Bible speaks of body and soul (or spirit), this was taken as a proof for the dichotomy doctrine. Some people were even more clever and came up with a *trichotomy* whereby humans are said to consist of three parts: body, soul, and spirit. Of course, 1 Thessalonians 5:23 ("May your whole spirit and soul and body be kept blameless at the coming of our Lord Jesus Christ") was adduced as evidence for this assertion, although this verse and all other proof texts never use terms like "consist of" or "parts."

I am not going into all the relevant Bible verses, because then my philosophical anthropology would change into a theological anthropology. Suffice it to say that the Bible knows nothing of Man "consisting of" several "parts." In the Bible, Man is always a unity, *not* an entity made up of a distinct body, a soul, and a spirit, which only secondarily are thought of as a unity. Moreover, in the Bible, words like *soul* and *spirit* have at least ten different meanings, ranging from purely biotic ones (breath, blood) to perceptive, sensitive, and spiritive meanings. In other words, the biblical usage of these terms is very differentiated. In many cases it is evident that only certain *immanent* meanings are implied.

Even when biblical language (implicitly) refers to Man as a transcendent being, several different terms are used, such as *soul* (Hebrew, *nefeš*; Greek, *psychē*), *spirit* (*rûah, pneuma*), *heart* (*lēb[ab], kardia*), and *kidneys* (sing., *kilyah, nephros*). Even *flesh* (*bāśār, sarx*) can be identified with the human Ego (Ps. 63:1). In the Bible, we find the same flexibility in its speaking about Man and his functioning as we find in everyday parlance. In philosophy and the sciences, we can work only with clear-cut, one-dimensional meanings. Do not expect them in the Bible! Every relevant term can have anywhere from several to numerous meanings. So do not try to combat my elementary presentation of a Christian philosophical anthropology with isolated Bible verses! I regard the Bible highly as the inspired Word of God. But I do not admire the Greek-Scholastic way in which many people—usually unconsciously—quote the Bible when it comes to anthropological matters. They quote only their own *selections*, and read their own phrases and terms—like "consisting of" and "parts"—into the Bible.

Fortunately, in the newer Reformed—more than in the Evangelical—theological literature, many authors have rejected both dichotomy and trichotomy. They have unmasked the Greek-scholastic manner in which the relevant Bible passages have usually been treated. We are not merely embodied souls nor animated corpses, or something like that. Human nature is not composed of a mundane body, somehow linked with a higher spirit. Rather, *all* our ways of being human are thoroughly corporeal and at the same time thoroughly spiritual (Gordon Spykman). Body, soul, and spirit are just different ways to look at Man as a whole.

The End of Dualism

Today, the Scholastic soul-body dualism—claiming that Man is composed of two parts, soul and body—may live on in certain fundamentalist circles, but it has become untenable. The same is even more true regarding trichotomy. We now know that, within cosmic reality, no psychical-spiritive activity of the Ego (the heart, the soul, the spirit, you name it) can occur apart from physical and physiological processes. Psychical and spiritive acts proceed from the transcendent Ego, and function in all immanent aspects of cosmic reality. There is no thinking, feeling, and willing without the influence of the physical constitution and the physiological activity of the body. There is no room anymore for the ancient idea of a material substance called the body. This idea has been replaced by dynamic, intensive interactions at the physical, biotic, psychical, and spiritive levels. Let me state it bluntly once more: even the deepest religious thoughts of your heart are not possible without an exchange of potassium and sodium ions on both sides of your brain cell membranes.

Do you realize what this implies? There is no longer any so-called "rational soul" that functions independently of physical processes. There is no longer even any "body substance" anymore, that is, some basic heap of matter that under all circumstances remains the same. Matter is no longer viewed as a substance, but as compressed energy. *There are no substances anymore.* Therefore, the whole attempt to read any form of substantialism (a dichotomy of two, a trichotomy of three substances, or whatever) into the Bible has become obsolete. It was a ventriloquistic way of dealing with God's Word: trying to have it utter Greek-pagan ideas!

Every kind of dichotomy (or trichotomy) consists of a *theoretical* separation between two (or three) immanent function complexes—for instance, a physical-biotic complex (the material body) and a psychical-spiritive complex (the rational, immortal soul). Such a separation is now known to be inconceivable because of the absolute mutual dependency and interwovenness not just of these two complexes, but of *all* immanent aspects and idionomies of human existence.

Over against all this substantialist thinking, we allow only for the distinction between, on the one hand, Man's immanent multi-sided functioning and, on the other hand, the transcendent, religious concentration point of this functioning, that is, the heart. *This is never a form of dualism*, because the functions are nothing but the ramifications of the heart itself, and the heart is nothing but the focal point of the functions themselves. The functions *are* the heart, namely, in its diversity; and the heart is the functions, namely, in their fullness and unity.

There is no place for any form of dualism here, although many authors have tried to accuse Christian philosophy of defending just another form of dualism. Distinguishing between P and Q does not necessarily involve a dualism. A dualism is involved only if P and Q are viewed as entirely separate and opposed to one another. But distinguishing between P and Q, while at the same time maintaining that P is nothing but Q in its fullness, and Q is nothing but P in its variety, can never be a dualism. Not a dualism but a monism, if you will.

Moreover, the precise relationship between the human Ego, on the one hand, and its whole immanent corporeal functioning, on the other hand, is at the profoundest level a mystery anyway. There is no science, no philosophy, not even theology, that can grasp this mystery. This is not mysticism, nor a form of disrespect for science. It simply means being aware of science's purposes and limitations. As the ancient thinkers said, Man is basically a *homo absconditus* (hidden Man). The essence of Man is just as much a mystery to him as God's essence is. And it is no wonder because the one was created in the image and likeness of the Other.

A New Approach

If this coherence between Man's immanent functioning and his transcendent heart is a mystery, we believingly have to accept this mystery. Only in this way will we correctly understand the fall of Man as well as his redemption. Sin in its deepest (transcendent) meaning is not merely a(n) (immanent) trespassing of some commandment, but affects the heart, and through the heart the whole of Man's immanent functioning. In considering this, we will avoid the Scholastic error of thinking that Man's reason was exempt from the consequences of the fall. Man's depravity is total, and this can best be grasped if we acknowledge the coherence between Man's immanent functioning and his transcendent heart. Similarly, also new birth, "regeneration," affects Man's heart, and through this the whole of his immanent existence. All human functioning within cosmic reality proceeds from an apostate heart governed by sin, or from a regenerated heart governed by the Holy Spirit (or, unfortunately, from a regenerated heart that is still dominated by sinful flesh; cf. Gal. 5:16-25).

In summary, we can say, firstly, that Christian philosophical anthropology resists all forms of functionalism, a term referring to the absolutization of certain immanent functions. The most dangerous of these functionalisms is rationalism, or the absolutization of human reason, the belief in the autonomy of reason. This is the view that Man is, above all, a rational being, that therefore the highest element in Man, his soul, is necessarily some rational soul, and that reason has remained more or less unaffected by the consequences of the fall. Over against this, we state that Man is not first and foremost a rational being, but a religious being. His *ratio* (reason) is just one of the many immanent functions of the transcendent heart.

Secondly, a Christian anthropology discerns all kinds of aspects and idionomies in immanent human existence, but at the same time recognizes that Man's inner being is not contained in any of these aspects and functions, and in any (substantialized) complex of immanent functions. Man's true being surpasses the whole of this immanent divergence, yet is never separated from it, nor would it ever dualistically stand over against this immanent functioning. I repeat: Man's heart is his functions, viewed in their fullness and unity, and his functions *are* his heart, viewed in its divergence and variety.

Thirdly, and perhaps most importantly, a Christian anthropology recognizes that there is no such thing as "Man in himself" (Man as such). Rather it claims that the whole being of Man can only be interpreted in terms of his relationship to his Origin, or in the case of paganism, to his alleged origin. *The highest knowledge that Man has of himself is religious self-knowledge*, knowledge before

God, knowledge of himself in the light of God's self-revelation. This never means that some "Man in himself" is, secondarily, related to God. On the contrary, this very relationship between Man and God—or since the fall, Man and his idols—belongs to the true being of Man. This is adequately expressed in the biblical picture of Man as the *image of God* (Gen. 1:26-27; 9:6; 1 Cor. 11:7; cf. 2 Cor. 4:4; Col. 1:15). Man is a *religious* being because of this inherent, existential orientation toward the ultimate ground of his being, that is, God or an alleged god.

Fourthly, true knowledge of Man is not possible through some Christian anthropology, no matter how profound. It is true *self*-knowledge, possible only through the regenerating power and enlightenment of the Holy Spirit in the *heart* of Man. It is self-knowledge through the operation of God's Word in the heart, through a living faith in the person and work of Jesus Christ with all one's *heart*, and through the unfolding expression of this in all Man's immanent functioning, from the logical to the pistical.

Marriage and Family

We have seen that Man's relation to God—or to the gods—belongs to his very being. It makes him a *religious* being in the profoundest sense of the word. Subservient to this is the fact that Man is, in addition to many other things, a *social* being. He cannot function other than in relationship with his surroundings: inanimate things, plants, animals, and in particular fellow human beings. Things, plants, and animals, function as objects within his human existence; they have object-functions in their relationship with Man. But Man's fellow human beings do not have any object-functions in their relationship to him. On the contrary, a relationship between one human and another human is one between subjects and subjects. Not only that, but these relationships, too, are essentially of a *transcendent* and *religious* nature because such relationships are *from heart to heart*, and always before God.

Traditionally, philosophical anthropology has focused too much on Man *per se*, as if such a being could ever exist. Man is null and void apart from his relationships, both the vertical one, with God (or the gods), and the horizontal one, with his fellow human beings. Both types of relationship belong to Man's very being. Man was created for a relationship with God in the first place, but in the second place, also for a relationship with others. In one and the same Bible passage, we are told that Man was created to be the image and likeness of God (vertical), but also to form the most intimate (horizontal) bond between two humans, namely, marriage (Gen. 1:26-28).

Marriage is a *natural* relationship; it is a given of God's creational order. Later in this chapter, we will come across other types of relationships, which are products of a historical process. In the terminology of our theory of modal aspects, we can say that marriage is *rooted* in the sexual relationship between a man and a woman, or that the *foundational* modality of marriage is the biotic one. But it would be a great mistake to think that the *destination* of marriage lies in the sexual bond. Only people like evolutionists and materialists could come up with such an idea. No, in Christian thinking it is the *ethical* function that describes the essence of marriage, that is, the love between husband and wife (Eccl. 9:9; Eph. 5:25, 28, 33; Col. 3:19; Titus 2:4).

Of course, a marriage functions in *all* modal aspects of cosmic reality. For instance, it has a sensitive aspect (the feelings which married persons have for each other), a logical aspect (you can reason about what constitutes a true marriage and what does not), a formative aspect (marriages differ from culture to culture, and from period to period), a lingual aspect (think of the various terms for marriages), a social aspect (marriage is one of many social bonds between people), an economic aspect (think of separate or joint ownership of property), an aesthetical aspect (think of [non-]harmony in marriage), a juridical aspect (what constitutes a marriage in the legal sense?) and a pistical aspect (marriage is intertwined with the beliefs of the two persons). But two aspects stand out: the biotic modality, which is the *foundational* one, and the ethical modality, which is the *destination* function of marriage.

Also the family in the limited sense, that is, two parents with their children, functions in all modal aspects. I name in particular the formative aspect (parents are supposed to educate their children), the lingual aspect (think of the confusion around families in the limited sense and the extended family, or of the parents' prerogative to give names to their children), the social aspect (except for childless marriages, the family is the smallest social unit within society), and the juridical aspect (e.g., the legal position of foster children and stepchildren). Again, two aspects stand out. The biotic modality is the *foundational* one because children and parents are all linked by the sexual relationships between the parents. The ethical modality is the *destination* function, because the family, too, is first and foremost a social group connected by love.

You might argue that small communities of friends living together also find their destination function in the ethical modality. That is true, but this relationship is not a *natural* one, that is, given as part of the creational order. Its foundational function is to be located in the formative (historical) modality.

The State

When we come to the societal relationships that are products of historical formation, we again have to make a fundamental distinction. Some historical societal relationships are direct *institutions* of God, other relationships are historical too, but are the free products of man's own cultural activity. Among the institutions of God, we distinguish two *natural* relationships: marriage and the family (see above), and two *historical* relationships: state and church.

Before the flood in the days of Noah, it is questionable whether the Bible implies anything that we would call a state (institutional government). But after the flood, the idea of a state, no matter how elementary, is clearly indicated: "Whoever sheds the blood of man, *by man* shall his blood be shed" (Gen. 9:6; italics mine). Please note the words "by man," and compare this with Genesis 4:15, where God says that no man is to kill Cain as a punishment for his murder of Abel. God's words to Noah imply some form of human authority for the first time, an elementary government that is entitled to implement the death penalty. With this institution of human government, no matter how elementary, we have the state in principle. Compare Romans 13:1-7, where, firstly, it is emphasized that governments are established by, and are servants of, God (vv. 1, 4). Secondly, the essence of the state is described as consisting in its right not only to make laws but also to apply the sword in order to maintain the law (v. 4).

Here we see that the *foundational* aspect is, as in all historical societal relationships, the formative one; states are always products of a historical process. But its *destination* function is the juridical one. Again I emphasize that the state functions in *all* modal aspects. Here are some examples: the social one (in a state, a number of citizens live together), the economic one (the state has its own budget), and the ethical one (the laws of the state are for the benefit of its citizens). But the true nature and destiny of a state lie in its juridical aspect.

The state has the responsibility of maintaining *public justice*. Think here of what I said about sphere sovereignty (chapter 3). The state is not supposed to meddle in the unique spheres of marriage, family, church, school, company, associations, etc. These are all sovereign within their own spheres. For instance, the state as such has nothing to say about what goes on in people's bedrooms, or how parents educate their children, about how schools teach pupils, about whether women are to be allowed in pulpits, etc. But the state does maintain public justice, so it does have something to say about husbands raping their wives, about parents or teachers abusing the children entrusted to them, about education in schools in terms of quality, about companies that operate illegally, etc.

Shortly after the Reformation, this was not yet clearly seen. In England, the king, as head of state, also became the head of the Church of England, and as such ordered a new Bible translation, the *King James Bible*. In the Netherlands, it was the States-General that convened the famous international Synod of Dort (1618-1619), and ordered a new Bible translation, the *Statenvertaling* (the States-General translation). Today, such a dominance of the state over church life would be unthinkable in any civilized country.

In the worst-case scenario, a state ruling over its citizens' private lives, their marriages, their churches, the way they educate children, a state that in fact owns all the schools and all the companies, is a dictatorial, and often even terrorizing system. It is totally against the Christian notion of the state as a strictly juridical system, which creates the necessary legal preconditions for an optimal functioning of societal life, but at the same time guarantees the freedom and unique responsibility of its citizens, individually as well as in their churches, schools, companies, etc.

The state can easily go wrong here. Socialism gives too much authority to the state, that is, gives it too many responsibilities that actually belong to the citizens. Liberalism does the opposite: it minimizes the state's authority, so that the state cares too little about those citizens who have great difficulty standing on their own feet (the weak, the sick, the aged, the disabled etc.), or have no other people to help them. In a Christian view of the state, a proper middle way has to be chosen.

The Church

In theology, many discussions have taken place about the question whether the church began with the regenerated Adam and Eve (Gen. 3), or whether it began on the day of Pentecost (Acts 2). That question is of no concern to the Christian philosopher as such. He does not even occupy himself with the church in a transcendent sense (the Body of Christ, which in him is seated in the heavenly places [Eph. 2:6]), or with the church in the sense of worldwide Christianity. No, what we are talking about is the church (small c!) as a local gathering of Christians, or the church as an interlocal or even international denomination. That is the church as a tangible phenomenon within immanent cosmic reality. And that this church is an institution of God is unquestionable.

Local churches and interlocal denominations are always products of historical processes, so the foundational aspect is again the formative one. It may be equally clear that their destination aspect lies in the pistical modality: churches and denominations are pistically qualified societal relationships. Of course, I emphasize again that a church functions in *all* modal aspects, for instance, a logical aspect (we can reason theologically about it), a lingual aspect (local churches and denominations have many different names), a social aspect (in each church, a number of Christians live together), an economic aspect (a church has its own budget), a juridical aspect (think of canon law), and an ethical aspect (Christians are supposed to live together in mutual love). But the true nature and destiny of a local church or an interlocal denomination lie in its pistical aspect. Churches and denominations are especially characterized by the fact that they share common beliefs.

We have seen that Man has immanent functions in all modal aspects, and at the same time transcends them. Similarly, churches and denominations have immanent functions in all modal aspects, but at the same time transcend them by being intertwined with the church as the Body of Christ, which surpasses time and the cosmos.

Here again, it is important to emphasize the meaning of sphere sovereignty. I said that the state should not rule over the church, but the opposite is also true: the church should not rule over the state. That was the case in medieval Roman Catholic Europe, where the church could condemn someone for (alleged) heresy, and then hand him over to the state to receive the death penalty. Today, that would be unthinkable in any civilized country.

Do not make a mistake here, though. The notion of sphere sovereignty does not mean that, apart from the church, societal relationships such as states, schools, companies, etc. are religiously neutral. There are no neutral people or neutral societal relationships. The state ought not to be under the authority of any denomination. But that does not alter the fact that people who exercise the state's authority are always religious people, whether they like it or not. That is, they stand before God as his servants (Rom. 13), whether they like it or not. They will have to give an account to him. The church does not have the monopoly on religion! All people are religious, that is, oriented toward their Ultimate Ground of certainty and confidence, whether this is God or some sort of idol. Therefore, not only churches but also states, schools, companies, associations, etc. are responsible to God.

Other Societal Relationships

We have found two natural, institutional societal relationships, namely, marriage and the family. We have also found two historical, institutional societal relationships, namely, the state and the church. Besides these, there are many other societal relationships, which do not have an institutional character but nevertheless are often a vital element in a civilized society. I mention the most important examples, and divide them by their spiritive destination functions:

Logical: e.g., scientific institutions and associations.

Formative: e.g., historical and technological associations.

Lingual: e.g., linguistic associations, such as those that want to maintain and promote certain minority languages.

Social: e.g., schools, social clubs, traffic organizations.

Economic: e.g., businesses, companies, firms, factories, banks.

Aesthetic: e.g., associations of artists, orchestras.

Juridical: e.g., tribunals, associations of lawyers.

Ethical: e.g., ethical associations.

Pistical: e.g., Bible clubs, synagogues, mosques, temples, but also political parties (the state is juridically qualified, a party is pistically qualified).

All these societal associations are neither natural, that is, given as part of the creational order, nor institutional, that is, based on divine institutions. Yet, quite a few of them are essential to a civilized society; in other words, they are the unavoidable outcome of historical processes in civilization. We could not imagine society without, in particular, scientific institutions, schools, companies, and tribunals. In that sense, the distinction between institutional and non-institutional relationships is only relative: marriage, family, church, and state have been *explicitly* instituted, but scientific institutions, schools, companies, and tribunals are *implicitly* given with the way God has put our world together.

Questions for Review

1. In what sense are the first four human idionomies unlike those of higher animals?

2. Explain what is meant by Man's spiritive idionomy.

4. In terms of human idionomies, why is it important that these are foundationally encapsulated within each other?

5. What does it mean that Man is both immanent and transcendent?

6. Explain the terms dualism, dichotomy, and trichotomy. Why is the phrase "transcendent Ego" better for describing Man's essence, instead of "soul" or "spirit"?

7. What is functionalism, and how does Christian philosophical anthropology resist it?

8. In the light of this chapter, what is the only path to true self-knowledge?

9. Provide a brief analysis, in terms of the modal aspects, of each of the following:
    • a human family
    • the state
    • the church

10. Give examples of the most important societal relationships, in terms of their spiritive destination functions.

Chapter Seven
A PHILOSOPHY OF SCIENCE

As I said in chapter 1, the philosophy of science could be called the "science about science," or the "theory about theories." That is, it is the theory about the nature, origin, and development of scientific theories. Every student of one of the special sciences should learn not only to investigate scientifically his field of study, but also to investigate scientifically the phenomenon of science as such. For instance, a junior psychologist should learn to distinguish between practical knowledge about humans and the theoretical investigation of psychical phenomena. A junior theologian should learn to distinguish between practical Bible knowledge and scholarly theology, or between a Bible college and a theological faculty.

Scientism

One of the snares into which the immature student can easily fall is *scientism*, that is, the overestimation of scientific thought and speech in comparison to practical, everyday thought and speech. This is also the error of overestimating science, including theology, in regard to the practical, everyday parlance of the Bible. For instance, it is claimed that science supplies us with more accurate information about cosmic reality than religion does (see below). Scientism is characterized by the following ideas:

1. *The strict separation between faith and science.* If this were correct, there would be no room at all for any distinctly Christian philosophy or science. Christianity and science would each be locked up in watertight compartments. This idea is quite characteristic of our present time, which has elevated science to be the highest source of knowledge and insight, and has pushed Christianity to the borders of society and confined it to the strictly private sphere. We call this secularization. At best, the Bible is considered to be some spiritual or mystical source of inspiration.

It is not a book that in any reliable way has relevance for culture, society, or politics, and certainly not for science.

2. *The idea of a neutral, objective, unbiased science.* It has to be said right away that, among philosophers of science, hardly anyone still seems to believe in this view, which is called *positivism.* Most of them are aware of the pre-scientific beliefs on which science is founded. However, among ordinary scientists—including theologians—who usually are not very interested in the philosophy of science, positivism still seems to be the common viewpoint, and this view is held even more so among the broad mass of non-scientists. Faith knowledge is considered to be biased, subjective, outdated; scientific knowledge is supposedly pure, trustworthy, and objective.

3. *The belief in the autonomy of reason.* This is the rationalistic view that sees human reason as autonomous, a term that means literally, "being its own law," subject to no higher authority, especially not to God and his Word. During the Renaissance (sixteenth century), and especially during the Enlightenment (eighteenth century), this view was strongly emphasized. In present day postmodernism, however, all Enlightenment views—rationalism, scientific optimism, the belief in continuous progression, etc.—are criticized. But ironically, this does not seem to hold for the autonomy of reason. This idea seems sacrosanct! By contrast, the Christian believes in the *theonomy* of reason. This does not mean that he follows different logical laws—on the contrary—but rather, that human thinking, in spite of its many liberties and options, is subject to God and his Word.

Biblioscientism

There is a special kind of scientism that I call *biblioscientism.* It is one of the characteristics of what we call today fundamentalism. This is a kind of scientism that is pursued not at the expense of the Bible but for the sake of the Bible. Ordinary adherents of scientism want to use so-called "neutral" science to prove the Bible wrong, whereas adherents of biblioscientism want to use that same so-called "neutral" science to prove the Bible right. Both appeal to allegedly solid facts and objective evidence to defend their respective cases. In other words, both start from the same positivistic error, because objective evidence does not exist. Both blame their opponent for starting from certain biases, over against which they themselves posit allegedly solid facts. However, facts are always facts-for-people; they function only within the framework of certain faith presuppositions, as we will see.

Adherents of biblioscientism claim that true science can never be in conflict with the Bible. This is a circular reasoning because they have already established what are the alleged facts of the Bible—often with little idea about proper exegesis and the hermeneutics of the Bible (the science of interpretation). They even read all sorts of modern scientific theories into the Bible, such as nuclear forces (Col. 1:17a; Heb. 1:3), the law of entropy (Gen. 3), isostasy (the equilibrium within the earth's crust; Isa. 40:12b), the field of gravity (Job 26:7b), the "red shift" in the spectrum of celestial bodies (Job 9:8a), photosynthesis (Deut. 33:14a), the fact that the moon has no light of its own (Job 25:5a), etc. Here the Bible's message is being degraded as scientific information. This is not only wrong, it is dangerous, because if these theories ever become obsolete, people will conclude that therefore the proof-texts involved will have been refuted as well.

Critical, Well-Founded Knowledge

In science (from the Latin, *scientia*, meaning knowledge) we try to gather knowledge. At a vocational school or in a spiritual education course, people also want knowledge, but that is not scientific knowledge. Not all knowledge is theoretical or scientific knowledge. The way in which knowledge is acquired and the nature of our knowledge must meet certain conditions if we want to speak of theoretical knowledge. To that end, let us compare some features of practical and theoretical knowledge.

Science never hovers in the air but always builds upon knowledge that already exists. This building process goes on forever. Knowledge is never finished or complete but always open to elaboration and extension. The scientist always has to account for this growing knowledge and for the sources of new knowledge. Every piece of knowledge that claims to be scientific must be based upon published scientific conclusions or upon the results of one's own scientific investigation. Knowledge that has no link with prior knowledge is no science. Amateurs sometimes think they have made some special discovery without realizing that in most cases, such work has been done before, or has even been refuted already.

In practical knowledge, such an accounting for acquired knowledge is often hardly possible or even necessary. We cannot check all the knowledge that we have acquired. That does not mean such practical knowledge is worthless. Remember that all scientific investigation has started from this practical knowledge. But practical knowledge is not very critical and often not very well founded.

For instance, on the basis of all his experience, a farmer can often tell us what weather we will have the next day, but he cannot easily account for this feeling. A meteorologist could never work in this way; he has to base his predictions on a coherent, well-established theory, which itself is based on many observations. (Nevertheless, the farmer sometimes gives a better prediction than the meteorologist!) In science we want reliable knowledge, that is, knowledge that is well founded and well defended on the basis of a long series of observations and experiments.

This does not mean, though, that theoretical knowledge is "higher" than practical knowledge; such an idea would belong to scientism. Much of practical knowledge surpasses reason, such as, for instance, the knowledge you have of your beloved. It is especially Christian philosophy that pays attention to forms of knowledge that are not rationally qualified. Do you really know your beloved only if your knowledge has to be critical, well founded, well argued? Is this knowledge not of a very different nature? Or think of the knowledge you have of God. This is not just theological knowledge (I hope); it is a knowledge that implies relationship, intimacy, and fellowship (John 17:3; cf. Gen. 4:1, Adam "knew" his wife).

Systematic, Coherent Knowledge

Practical knowledge is often acquired in a spontaneous, arbitrary, and largely subconscious way. As a consequence, it is fragmentary and incoherent. That is no problem if you need this knowledge only for, say, some practical skill, like playing the piano (you do not have to understand the mechanics of the piano or know all music theory) or driving a car. Scientific knowledge, however, ought, as much as possible, to form a systematic, coherent whole. There is no place for loose pieces of knowledge; if they occur, they have to be integrated in the whole, or discarded. Moreover, science usually acquires its knowledge not in a spontaneous, arbitrary way but in an orderly, purposeful manner through systematic investigation, that is, observation and experimentation. The results of this investigation are represented in theories in which the various observations have been organized with a logically meaningful coherence.

Again, I emphasize that this holds only for rational types of knowledge. I repeat, it is especially Christian philosophy that pays attention to forms of knowledge that are not rationally qualified, such as knowledge in relationships: knowledge of God, knowledge of one's beloved. Or take another example: aesthetic knowledge, that is knowledge of the beautiful, the harmonious. It is typical of rationalistic thought that, because knowledge of the beautiful and the ugly cannot be conceptualized (rationally locked up in concepts), it is often treated as something subjective and arbitrary. The philosophical school of logical positivism has even marked the aesthetic, together with the ethical, as non-knowledge. But how can we explain that everyone who knows classical music agrees that Bach and Mozart are among the greatest composers ever, or that everyone who knows the arts agrees that Rembrandt and Caravaggio were some of the most outstanding painters? If this is non-knowledge, how can there be such a consensus? There *must* be objective criteria for art even if these criteria are very difficult to conceptualize.

In itself, the demand that scientific knowledge must be critical, systematic, and objective is not sufficient. A technician who searches for some malfunction in a car does so in a systematic and objective way, but what he does is not physics or engineering science. A judge who has to pass a verdict collects his data in a critical and systematic way and uses responsible objective methods. But neither the technician's nor the judge's study is of a scientific nature. Although the work of both presupposes a lot of scientific theory, this does not make their work itself scientific work. It is of a *practical* nature: the car has to move again, the accused has to be locked up or released. It is not of a *theoretical* nature, that is, aimed at augmenting our scientific knowledge as a purpose in itself.

Detached, Unconcerned Knowledge

In our practical approach to cosmic reality we always understand the cosmos in its integral totality, just as the Creator has given it to our experience. This approach is concrete and immediate; it lacks the typical cool distance with which the scientist observes reality. The word *practical* comes from the Greek verb *prattō*, which means "to act, to do." The word *theoretical* comes from the Greek verb *theaomai*, which means "to behold"; the word *theatre* comes from the same root. In the theatre we "behold" ("see," "consider") the things that happen on the stage. We may be emotionally concerned about these events, yet there is always a distance; we are not *part* of these events. In the same way, the scientist may be emotionally concerned about his field of investigation. Yet, he remains at a cool distance, for he is never to lose his objectivity in the sense that his results will not be distorted by his affections or emotions.

The difference between the practical and the theoretical approach to reality is the difference between the way a loving dog owner looks at his dog, and the way a biologist looks at a dog that functions as a subject for his experiments. The former sees a concrete animal, with which he maintains a close bond. The latter does not want a bond with the animal, because he does not want to lose the appropriate distance from his experiments. For the same reason, most doctors do not like to operate on their own spouses; they would not be able to maintain the appropriate distance from the physical body being operated on. Because of this difference between the practical and the theoretical approach, a person could be an excellent educator who nevertheless raises his own children badly. Similarly, he could be an excellent economist but administer the finances of his own household very badly.

Christian philosophy again raises the question here whether scientific biology is "higher" than practical knowledge of nature. It is only higher than *rational* practical knowledge of nature but not higher than the comprehensive, immediate knowledge the dog owner has of his dog. Psychology is not higher than the knowledge of a good pastor regarding the members of his congregation. Musicology or literary theory is not higher than the heart warming, even ecstatic knowledge one may have of Monteverdi or Shakespeare. One has to be an obstinate rationalist to claim the contrary.

Analytical, Abstract Knowledge

The example of the dog lover and the biologist can help us understand another difference between practical and theoretical knowledge. The dog owner experiences his dog as a totality. In our Christian-philosophical terminology: all the dog's modal aspects are equally important, and no single aspect stands out. The owner may become conscious of a certain aspect at a certain moment, for instance, when the dog is in heat (biotic), or has to be sold (economic), or participates in a dog show (aesthetic), or has been stolen (juridical). But even in these cases, it is always the whole dog that is involved. With the biologist, this is different. As a biologist, he leaves the economic, the aesthetic, the juridical, and all the other aspects out of consideration, and concentrates exclusively on the biotic aspect.

Science does not only limit itself to a single field of investigation, for instance dogs, but also considers its object of study from one single modal viewpoint only. This viewpoint is abstracted from the whole of the study object. I have explained this extensively in chapter 3. I tried to point out that, strictly speaking, the special sciences are never concerned with concrete phenomena as such, but always with certain aspects (e.g., the physical, biotic, sensitive, logical, social, economic, aesthetic, juridical, ethical aspects) of phenomena. In other words, science is based upon a *modal analysis* of reality, that is, an analysis according to one of a few modal points of view.

Again, Christian philosophy emphasizes that theoretical knowledge is not higher than practical knowledge. Why would a form of knowledge that considers only *one* modal aspect of a study project to be superior than the knowledge that views this project as a *whole*? People think this is so because it turns out that a modal analysis of reality has deepened our insight enormously in that specific modal side of reality. This tremendous success may suggest some superiority of scientific knowledge, but this is misleading. Modal analysis can never be an aim in itself; it is only a means to an end, namely, the deepening and clarification of our practical knowledge, our supra-rational knowledge of reality in particular, in the light of God's revelation. This is the highest knowledge. In order to deepen *this* knowledge, theoretical knowledge is a fantastic aid—but nothing more. It is a servant, not a queen. The earth trembles under "a servant who displaces her mistress" (Prov. 30:23).

Objective, Reproducible Knowledge

Practical knowledge is closely linked to the individual. Each person has his own unique and specific collection of practical knowledge, dependent on his personal history and experiences. In science, this is very different. Scientific knowledge is never the scientist's own private property but always the possession of a scientific *community*. A strictly personal science, which actually cannot be done by anyone else other than the discoverer, is no true science at all.

This collective character of science implies that, in principle, it does not matter who carries out the experiment. Sure, the inventor of a whole new experimental project that leads to magnificent results becomes famous. But if later investigators were to conduct the same experiments and produce very different results, his fame would dwindle very quickly. Different investigators doing the same experiment should come to approximately the same results; in other words, experiments should be *reproducible*. This involves the demand for *objectivity*. It is always highly desirable if scientists check one another's scientific results.

Science can never be objective in the sense of having no presuppositions, no pre-scientific beliefs upon which it is founded. However, science *does* need to be objective when it comes to obtaining reliable results. No scientist is to slant or adapt his results because the effects suit him better. Sometimes this kind of objectivity has been called "inter-subjectivity": different scientists doing the same scientific work should come to similar results.

This does not hold only for the experimental sciences, but also for the humanities. Scholars consulting the same literary sources or studying the same situation (event, state of affairs) should come to comparable results. Even if a situation is unique, it is never unique in every respect; there are always connections with other events or states of affairs. For instance, Leonardo da Vinci's *Mona Lisa* is a unique painting, yet a painting like thousands of other paintings, and as such, subject to artistic criteria that help us establish what *kind* of painting it is (a Renaissance portrait), and whether it is a mediocre painting or an exceptionally good one.

Criteria of Science

Summarizing what I said above, we conclude that true science is a human activity that, in a critical and systematic way, forms theoretical knowledge about a field of investigation by means of modal analysis, in such a way that this knowledge is well founded, coherent, objective (non-investigator-dependent) and reproducible. Science that is not critical, systematic, well founded, and reproducible is no true science—but these criteria, though essential, are not sufficient (see above, about the technician and the judge). Only two criteria are essential *and* sufficient; these are the criteria of theoretical distance and modal analysis. They are not found in the work of the technician or the judge because their work is of a *practical* nature, has a *practical* purpose, is not aimed at deepening theoretical insight, and is characterized by immediate concern with the subject involved and by a multilateral experience, that is, without modal abstraction.

Similarly, the arts, religion, skillfulness, etc. are not sciences because they do not aim at deepening our scientific knowledge. Aesthetics (sciences of the arts), theology (or psychology of religion), engineering sciences, etc. *are* sciences, for they aim at deepening our theoretical insight into the arts, into religion, and various skills, respectively. However, it would be a typically scientistic error to assert that aesthetics is higher than the arts themselves, or the science of religion higher than religion, with the argument that aesthetics and the psychology of religion are sciences, while art and religion are not. One painting by Vincent Van

Gogh is worth more than all the wisdom of aesthetics concerning it, although this painting is not scientific. And an inspiring Christian encounter is worth infinitely more than all the wisdom of the psychology of religion concerning it.

The theory of the modal aspects sheds some light on this problem. Science is about observation and theoretical insight; that is, the perceptive and the logical modalities stand out here. In the arts, however, it is the aesthetic modality that stands out, and if you like, also the sensitive modality within the admirer of them. The arts represent reality in their own characteristic way, just as science does this in its own characteristic way. The various religions represent reality in their own characteristic, always pistically qualified ways. Any particular way of representation is not necessarily higher or better than another (as long as we do not confuse the various religions with the faith in God within the reborn heart). I will return to this important matter in the last chapter.

Science and Abstraction

Earlier in this chapter, I spoke about abstraction as a characteristic of theoretical thought. Perhaps the most important type of abstraction in science is *modal* abstraction: every special science has its own modal viewpoint from which it studies cosmic reality. I have described this extensively in chapter 3.

A second form of abstraction in science has been described by Hendrik van Riessen as the *abstraction of the universal*. That is, the unique elements in an event are disregarded; the scientist searches for what events of a similar nature have in common. What is the *universal* element in the event or in the state of affairs under investigation? In fact, this means searching for the *laws* that hold for these similar events. For instance, think of the Law of Gay-Lussac, which says that the product of the pressure and the volume of a gas, divided by its temperature, is constant. This law is always valid, irrespective of place and time, or the mood of the investigator, or the kind or the amount of gas that is used. The physicist likes to speak here of the "ideal gas," from which all the peculiar features of the various gases have been abstracted (disregarded), so that the universal features, those that make a gas a gas, remain.

All sciences know such laws, although in the humanities they are more difficult to point out than in the natural sciences, and often they are not even called laws. Yet, sociology knows such laws (what rules help best to preserve social bonds?), economics knows them (such as the law of supply and demand), aesthetics knows them (what makes great music great music?), jurisprudence knows them (punishment must be proportionate to the crime committed), etc. (See chapter 4 for further examples).

A third form of abstraction in science is *experimental abstraction*, which is characteristic of experiments. An experiment is an artificial set-up in which a certain variable is observed under controlled conditions. The influence of all other possible variables is abstracted (taken away), such that only the single variable that is to be investigated remains. If a variable y is a function of the variables p, q and r, and we want to measure the influence of p, we must keep q and r constant, and vary p, etc. So, for the time being, q and r are abstracted from the experimental situation.

Abstraction of the objective involves abstracting not only the irrelevant factors in an observational situation but also those within the investigator himself; his mood, his eagerness, his personal views, and his experience are not to influence his results. Only the logical faculty is to remain active. Of course, sensitive, social, economic and moral factors cannot be taken away from him, but through intensive training he should learn to switch off these factors during the investigation. This does not mean he is not allowed to be overjoyed when his investigation yields positive results (sensitive), or that strong bonds within his team are forbidden (social), or that he is not to be thrifty when considering purchasing new equipment (economic), or that no moral considerations are allowed (ethical). On the contrary. The point is, however, that none of these factors is to affect his *results* or his *theories*.

In each scientific investigation, two modal aspects stand out: the logical aspect within the investigator, and the modal aspect, varying from the arithmetical to the pistical, of the object of study. For instance, in biology, the logical aspect of the biologist stands over against the biotic aspect of cosmic reality; in sociology, the logical aspect of the sociologist stands over against the social aspect of cosmic reality, and so on.

To be sure, abstraction as such is not an exclusive characteristic of theoretical thought. It is just as much a characteristic of practical thought. Every conceptualization is based on abstraction. The concept of a chair contains all features that are characteristic of all chairs, whereas all non-specific elements (size, materials, color, etc.) are abstracted from it. This is the abstraction of *things*. There is also the abstraction of *properties*: red is the feature that all red things have in common, good the common feature of all good things, beautiful the common feature of all beautiful things. This kind of abstraction occurs in everyday life. A painter may think about redness, a jury member about goodness. But only when a physicist thinks about redness in electromagnetic terms (physical aspect), or when an ethicist studies deeper criteria for good and bad (ethical aspect), do we enter into the theoretical domain.

Strictly speaking this theoretical thinking starts already at primary school, namely, when a child learns to calculate. It is a big leap from two apples plus two apples is four apples (practical-concrete) to the notion that $2 + 2 = 4$. Here, the arithmetical is abstracted from concrete reality as an aim in itself, to help the child discover the intricacies of the arithmetical modality (though not in these terms, of course). From there, the child returns to practical life, for in practice we never calculate abstractly, since we always add concrete things: two dollars plus two dollars (or cows, or persons, or houses, etc.). He who knows how much $2 + 2$ is, also knows how much two dollars plus two dollars is. In this way, theoretical abstractions are applied practically in everyday life. A theory is never an end in itself but a means to make practical life more livable. From abstraction back to the concrete! We will return to this important point in the last chapter.

Practical Observation

There can be no science without observation, except mathematics—and even mathematicians would hardly know about circles if they were not familiar with round things in practical life. In the twentieth century, philosophers—Dooyeweerd was one of the first—began to realize ever more clearly that this observation can never be neutral or objective, that is, unbiased. In the first place, in each (practical) observation a certain "cognitive structuring" occurs, that is, our observation is structured by our previous knowledge (cognition) that we possess with respect to the facts observed. What does this mean?

When we observe a fact (from Latin *factum*, made, done, happened), this observation is not just an "objective" bunch of *sense data*, as positivism asserted. Sense data are "sensations" of shapes and colors, sounds, smells and tastes. If we observe a bird, for example, we believe that this observation refers to the objective (i.e., observer-independent) reality of the bird. But observation of an objective bird does not imply an objective observation of the bird. The observed shapes, colors, and sounds together do not yield a bird. Without some knowledge of birds in general, of different bird species, of the nature, structure, ways of flying, and other habits of birds, we would not see a bird, but only the distinct shapes and colors.

In Christian philosophy, we would say that you need some practical knowledge of the idionomies (structural laws) that make a bird a bird (see chapter 5). Science helps us discover the laws that hold for cosmic reality, but the opposite is true as well: without some basic, practical knowledge of idionomies (structural laws), in this case, of a bird, you would never be able to see birds. Our previous cognition of birds, that is, of the structural laws that make birds to be birds, does structure the sensations we receive when we watch a bird. Our eyes see colors and shapes; it is our consciousness that, because of this cognitive structuring, sees a bird. Therefore, *perception* (in our consciousness) is more than a totality of *sensations* (through our sense organs); it is at least sensations-plus-cognitive-structuring. Only those who have learned what a paprika taste is, will taste paprika in a certain dish, whereas the ignorant person does not taste anything peculiar.

Even the sensations of shapes, colors, sounds, smells and tastes are not, however, cognition-independent sense data. The sensation of a red color would be experienced very differently if everything around us were red, or if we were not cognizant of the concept "red." We see orange because the term *orange* belongs to our vocabulary. There are nations that have no word for *orange* and therefore do not see orange; invariably they see reddish yellow, or yellowish red.

Twentieth-century philosophy has placed great emphasis on the meaning of language, also within science. Our concepts are little windows to reality. We are not able to observe the things for which we have not developed concepts and names. I would not see a horse if I did not know beforehand the concept "horse" as well as the word "horse" for that concept. I might see an animal because I was familiar with the concept "animal" beforehand. But without some knowledge of horses I would not recognize the animal as a horse.

Language is like a net that is cast over reality. That which can be caught in that net is that which language can handle. I literally do not see much when I watch a cricket match or an American football game because I hardly know the rules and aims of these games. (Sorry!) In the jungle I would not see very much either, whereas natives would see a hundred times more because they know the jungle. There is no knowledge without previous perception; but neither is there any true perception without some previous knowledge. That is how an infant learns to see, that is, to move from pure sensations to true perception: by gradually learning by what kind of things he or she is surrounded. The more the baby knows, the more the baby will perceive—and the more the baby perceives, the more the baby will know. The two go hand in hand all the time.

"Laden" Sensations

There is more than just cognitive structuring. If we were to pay attention only to the cognitive aspect, we might easily end up back in rationalism. Besides being loaded with our previous cognition, our sensations are laden with many memories, experiences, positive and negative affections, emotions, (right or wrong) ideas, our imagination, our will, etc. How different are the ways a mother, a teacher, a youth worker, a slave trader, a pedophile, a judge at a juvenile court, etc. look at one and the same child. Or rather, it is never the same child. How differently do we see a certain child after we have heard that he or she is extremely bright, or is a malicious thief, or has been seriously abused by his or her parents. No child is ever an objective fact. As I said before, facts are always facts-for-people. It is not the sense data of a fact that make it a fact, but *your* perception—that is, sensations plus cognition, memories, affections, etc.—turns the received sensations into a multi-sided fact-for-you.

We can now better explain the erroneous character of fundamentalist biblioscientism, which attempts to read solid scientific facts into the Bible (see above). The biblical facts, too, function only within a certain cognitive context, which in this case is strictly pistically qualified. That is, the Bible always speaks the language of faith; it is never interested in natural or historical data as such. When such data are mentioned, it always occurs in the context of faith, not of science or historiography. Scripture is divinely reliable, not because it turns out to be scientifically correct but because, also where it speaks about nature and history, it comes from, and refers back to, him who is the Truth. As such, Scripture primarily addresses our heart and our faith, rather than our scientific curiosity.

Practical versus Theoretical Observation

One might suppose that a scientist observes facts in a much more objective way than the practical observer. To a certain extent, this is true because he has to exclude his (positive or negative) affections, his imagination, his will (which shows him what he *wants* to see), as well as he can. However, scientific observation, too, is necessarily cognitively structured. In this case, we are dealing with a special type of cognition, namely, theoretical knowledge. Scientific observation is always theory-laden, that is, it always occurs in a theoretical context.

Philosophers of science usually claim that *all* observation, including practical observation, is theory-laden. In this case, cognitive structuring and theory-ladenness amount to the same thing, in that all cognition is theoreticalized (turned into something theoretical). However, long before theoretical thought was invented, people knew what birds or children were. These practical forms of observation and knowledge do not involve any biological or other theories. In Christian philosophy, we speak of theory-laden observation only when, for instance, a biologist observes a bird in a detached, systematic way, from a strictly biotic point of view, or a lawyer observes a child in a detached, systematic way from a strictly juridical point of view.

This blurring of the difference between practical and theoretical knowledge is a consequence of rationalism and scientism, whose central claim is that true knowledge is theoretical knowledge. This blurring can be observed everywhere. People assert that every (thinking) human is an armchair philosopher—as if our practical worldview is something of a philosophical cosmology. Or people claim that every person is an armchair psychologist because we constantly form theories about our fellow men—as if our practical impressions of our fellow men could be theoreticalized that easily. These impressions are not even faintly like psychological theories. The practical judgment of people is very different from any type of anthropology, just as practical faith knowledge of the Bible is radically different from theological theories (see the next chapter).

Of course, theoretical concepts and ideas also permeate modern Man's everyday, practical knowledge. But that does not make everyday knowledge a condition that is theory-laden. Let no psychological theories come between you and your beloved, and let no theological theories come between you and your God! Scientific (biological, psychological, historical, sociological) knowledge about women in general has very little to do with the relationship between my wife and me. Similarly, theological theories have very little to do with your knowledge of, and fellowship with, God.

Theoretical Observation

Natural scientists in particular supply us with many examples of the theory-ladenness of their observations. Although they are called natural scientists, physicists and chemists in particular, hardly ever observe phenomena in nature. Their observation involves only the position of pointers in measuring instruments, colors of chemical color indicators, etc. (Ernst Mach). Such instruments and color indicators are based on complicated theories. In other words, the correctness of the observations involved depends on the correctness of the underlying theories. The observations are theory-laden in the sense that they are embedded in these theories, so to speak.

These theories have given rise to the experiments we are talking about. That is, these experiments have the purpose of testing the predictions that have been made on the basis of these theories. This is an important point: not only do observations lead to theories, but theories lead to observations, as Karl Popper has emphasized. To be sure, in science there are hardly any theories that are not based on observations. But it is equally true that there are hardly any scientific observations that are not based on preceding theories. Scientific observations are not only theory-laden but also theory-inspired. It is naïve to think—as the British philosopher of science, Francis Bacon, did in the sixteenth century—that scientific work is one-way traffic, that is, from observation to theory; there is just as much traffic moving from the other direction!

Theoretical Entities and Laws

A (scientific) theory can be understood as a kind of framework in which a large number of observations have been put together, a framework that supplies us with certain views about the coherence between these observations. A vital element in these views is the *laws* that are assumed to account for the observations; think of what I said earlier about the "abstraction of the universal." Observations are interpreted in terms of certain laws that have been formulated for a certain kind of phenomena. Event P happens because there is a law Y that predicts that in a given situation P *must*, or *will probably*, happen.

Phenomena can also be explained in terms of certain *theoretical entities*. These entities have never been observed in a direct way but have been postulated to explain certain observations. For instance, no one has ever seen an electron or a gene (at most, we have seen pictures, which, *on the basis of certain theories,* are interpreted as representing molecules or genes). In spite of this, we assume their existence, because numerous phenomena can be very conveniently explained through them. We consider a phenomenon to be explained if we can show that it is nothing but a specific example of a more general law Y or phenomenon Z.

Thus, sound is explained by referring to the phenomenon of air vibration, neuroses are explained in terms of suppression and other defense mechanisms, unusual features in organisms are explained in terms of mutated genes, the decline of dialects is explained from the dominance of the national language, etc.

Inductive sciences are sciences that, on the basis of a large number of individual cases, try to arrive at general rules (laws) to explain them. This movement from the specific to the general is called *induction*. Subsequently, on the basis of these general laws new specific cases can be explained. That is, from cases A, B, C, and D, general rule P is derived; subsequently, E and F are explained by rule P.

Deductive sciences, such as mathematics and logic, follow the opposite pathway. They start with certain general theses that are considered to be self-evident or which cannot be defended any further; they have the status of axioms. From these general theses, specific theses are derived.

Induction in the broadest sense can be described as the attempt to explain the *factual side* (or *subject-side*) of cosmic reality in terms of the *law-side* of reality (see extensively chapter 4). In their own way, the deductive sciences, too, try to get a grasp of the law side of reality. This seems to be a general underlying question of all types of sciences: what are the laws that govern our world, from the mathematical to the pistical world? All the special sciences can be explained as attempts to unveil the law-order that the Creator has instituted for cosmic reality (even if the scientists involved would not like to put it that way). And it is one of the tasks of philosophy to investigate and interpret this state of affairs: it tries to unveil the law-order as it applies to scientific activity.

Questions for Review

1. What is scientism, and what ideas characterize it?

2. What is biblioscientism, and why is it dangerous to use the Bible to "prove" a scientific theory?

3. What are some differences between scientific knowledge and practical knowledge? Why are these differences significant?

4. What is "true science"?

5. Identify and explain three kinds of abstraction relating to scientific knowledge.

6. Identify and explain the kinds of abstraction involved in practical knowledge.

7. What does it mean that practical knowledge often precedes, and is a prerequisite for, theoretical knowledge?

8. What does it mean that scientific observation is always theory-laden?

9. What is meant by induction? By deduction? What role do they play in science?

Chapter Eight

SCIENCE AND WORLDVIEWS

In chapter 1, I pointed out the importance of the term "world-view." A worldview has an intermediate function between our scientific work, on the one hand, and the faith attitude of our hearts, on the other hand. In brief, the differences between these three could be formulated as follows: science is rational and theoretical, a worldview is rational and practical, and faith is supra-rational and practical.

A worldview is an aggregate of fundamental convictions with respect to the world—cosmic reality—and is determined by what we have described as "religious ground-motives." Sometimes people speak of a "view of life," but perhaps it is better to define a view of life as an aggregate of fundamental convictions with respect to the nature, meaning, and purpose of human life. A worldview is a more encompassing notion; a view of life is only part of it.

In the description of a worldview as I have just given it, a number of features are included, which I am going to work out below. Again, the theory of modal aspects can be of great help here. I will limit myself to some of the most outstanding modal aspects, and I challenge the reader to work out the other spiritive aspects of worldviews for himself.

The Sensitive Aspect

A worldview is not just a set of rational beliefs concerning the world. It also involves how you "feel" about the world, how you are "moved" by it, how you "feel" about your relationship to the world. A lot of elements in our worldview have more to do with positive and negative affections and with—sometimes very strong—emotions than with strictly rational considerations. To a great extent, a worldview develops in a person through positive and negative experiences, or good and bad memories, which lead to positive and negative affections. For instance, your attitude towards religion might have less to do with rational arguments, and more with good or bad experiences in the church you went to, good or bad memories of your religious education (at home, at school), and things like that.

The sensitive aspect also entails the fact that a worldview is a driving power in a person's life. I have explained before that a religious ground-motive is something that drives one's heart, and this is a transcendent matter. But there is certainly an immanent element in this driving, which is of a sensitive nature. Arising from the heart, a worldview motivates a person's speaking and acting in his concrete everyday life, such as in his human relationships, his lifestyle, his education, his social and political actions, his cultural activities, his science and his philosophy. In all these matters his worldview is the driving force ("force" being here an analogy with the energetic modality). The word *motivate* comes from the Latin *movere*, "to move," movement being here an analogy with the kinematic modality.

What moves you? What drives you? What are the things you feel strongly about? The answer is most simply given by describing your beliefs, your worldview. Are you moved by the misery of the persecuted, or of many women in this world, or of ill-treated animals? Are you driven by the misery of the poor and the weak in our society? By the poverty in communist countries, or in capitalist countries, for that matter? By the rise of atheism and materialism? By the decline of Christianity in the Western world, and the concomitant loss of Bible knowledge? Or, to be honest, are you driven by your hobby-horses and your idiosyncrasies? There must be something that really touches you, and drives you to action. Most people have ideals, which to a great extent are of a sensitive nature.

The Logical Aspect

Every human being is, among many other things, a logical being, that is, a thinking being. He cannot help thinking about the mysteries of life and of this world, even if ever so superficially. Many people have at least vague, and often quite outspoken, foundational convictions about the most profound questions of life and of this world. These foundational convictions constitute ideas about the origin, meaning, destination, purpose, and value of Man and the world, and about the mutual relationships between humans and fellow-humans, between Man and society, between Man and his environment, between Man and his God, or god, or gods.

Of course, the thinking of some persons about these things is very shallow. Actually, they seem to be hardly interested in the basic questions. However, this is only apparently the case. In certain borderline situations (heavy illness, divorce, substantial losses, dying), many people do turn out to have certain definite ideas about what really matters in life. And even if people only (seem to) live for money, for sex, for sports, for music or other pleasures, they do have some idea about the meaning of life, no matter how poor this idea may be in other people's eyes.

Another reason why the worldviews of many people are poorly developed is that a coherent worldview is not at all popular in our postmodern time. Postmodernism has no room for "grand narratives" (See above in chapter 2). The phrase "grand narrative" (*grand récit*) stems from the twentieth-century French philosopher, Jean-François Lyotard, and means an encompassing and coherent view in which all facets of reality find their interpretation. It seems that today there is little interest in such comprehensive, all-interpreting worldviews.

However, is this really so very different from the situation in the modern period, that is, the period preceding our postmodern time? How many people ever had a truly comprehensive and fully consistent worldview? In practice, the worldviews of most people consist only of bits and pieces, often without much coherence. Yet we may expect—and hope—that intellectuals who are especially interested in philosophy or some special science have more or less articulated views about Man and society, history and culture, meaning and purpose.

The Formative Aspect

A worldview is not a static aggregate of beliefs but always has a dynamic dimension. In the life of the individual, a worldview changes as the person acquires more knowledge and more experience, which usually means more maturity and more practical wisdom.

One could almost say that, although certain foundational convictions usually remain the same, in every new stage of life the individual has a renewed worldview. Similarly, the worldview of an entire community (see next section) and an entire culture renews itself constantly, whether traditionalists like it or not. Such a worldview grows and changes in a natural, often unnoticed (unconscious) way according to the demands of the successive time periods, and according to new potentials given with the new times. New ideas arise, which usually affect, or even replace, the existing worldviews.

The central religious ground-motive in which a certain worldview is rooted determines what is variable and what is permanent. The Christian, too, who finds his starting point in the Word of God, will have to distinguish between the timeless creational ordinances that are taught, often implicitly, by the Word, and the time-bound applications of these ordinances in different time periods. Often, such applications are found also in Scripture, or at least in one's own denominational tradition. In a Christian worldview, the timeless creational ordinances are in principle undebatable. But the things that *are* debatable are the time-bound applications of them, as well as—I have to add—the question what exactly belongs to these creational ordinances, and what does not.

This is a difficult and ongoing discussion. On the one hand, the revolutionary tries to overthrow the timeless creational ordinances. That is wrong. On the other hand, the reactionary traditionalist clings to certain time-bound applications of these ordinances. That is wrong, too. The problem is that, for the latter, these outdated applications *are* timeless creational ordinances. In this way, slavery has been defended with an appeal to Genesis 9:25, the poverty of laborers with an appeal to Deuteronomy 5:11 or Matthew 26:11, and racial segregation has been defended with an appeal to Deuteronomy 32:8 or Acts 14:16. Have we become wiser in the meantime, or do we still adhere to certain time-bound applications?

The Social Aspect

In a certain sense, every worldview is unique in that no two persons have exactly the same views of all aspects of life. Globally speaking, however, a worldview is never the possession of an individual but of the community to which he belongs. Thus, a worldview also has an important social aspect. A person is a member of a family, a nation, a church community, a cultural community, etc. Communities have their own specific histories and aspirations, and are historically marked by specific religious, ideological, and political convictions. Along with this, they develop their own specific worldviews. These worldviews stamp a certain societal relationship, such as a family, a state, a school, a political party, as Christian, liberal, socialist, conservative, communist, materialist, nihilist, etc.

Worldviews have a universal character because (1) every human has a certain view of the world, and because (2) many scientists especially have a view of every important facet of the world. That is, *everyone* has a worldview, and some people even have a worldview about *everything*. That is universal in a double sense.

People who have certain convictions grow up in, or look for, communities with similar worldviews. They are not just satisfied with their own worldview but wish to belong to, or join, communities where they can feel at home. This also holds for scientists: they could not work anywhere else than in a community that shares the same paradigm, that is, the same scientific and pre-scientific framework of thought. Scientists who have different worldviews can often cooperate very well within a team. But on some essential points, their worldviews have to overlap; in order to work together they need this common paradigm, a common framework, in which they have been socialized in similar universities. For someone who does not accept this paradigm, there is no place at the university, nor on a scientific team. In this respect, the scientific world can be as sectarian as certain church denominations!

Think of contemporary philosophers who currently rank among the stars, including Noam Chomsky, Daniel Dennett, and Martha Nussbaum (all three from the USA), Charles M. Taylor (Canada), Jürgen Habermas and Peter Sloterdijk (both from Germany), John Gray (UK), and others. They all share the typical values of Western society. Even a great philosopher like Amartya Sen from India functions within the Western thought climate. They may be conservative (Gray), anti-capitalist (Chomsky), or postmodernist (Sloterdijk), but they basically share the same post-Enlightenment tradition. No matter how different and original you may be, no matter how you may criticize your own tradition, you are always part of a community. You can never be a true philosopher or scientist on your own.

The Pistical Aspect

There could hardly be a worldview that lacks any notion about the existence and meaning of God or the gods (idols), or about the relationships of the cosmos to them. You may be an adherent of Judaism like Nussbaum, or a Roman Catholic like Taylor, or a staunch atheist like Dennett, but you nevertheless *do* have some ideas about God. Atheists live by the grace of theists: if there were no theists, atheists would have nothing to deny or combat. And if the atheist denies there is a god, he at least has an alternative conviction that, for him, functions as the Ultimate Ground of his convictions, as Darwinism seems to function for Dennett.

The pistical modality is concerned with what we call "religion" in everyday life (Dutch: *godsdienst*); think of religious objects, actions, events, professions, communities, etc. They are all pistically qualified, that is, they find their true character and purpose in the pistical modality. This is not to be confused with religion (Dutch: *religie*) in its transcendent meaning. Not every person adheres to a particular religion, but every (thinking) person is religious in the transcendent sense I described before, that is, he or she is a person who has an ultimate commitment. This is the same difference as the one we dealt with in previous chapters, the difference between faith in its immanent meaning, as a set beliefs that can be rationally accounted for, and faith in its supra-rational, transcendent meaning: faith as the existential ground-attitude of the human heart. We can define a worldview as a set of (rational, immanent) beliefs, rooted in a person's (supra-rational, transcendent) faith. A worldview has a rational—or not so rational—nature but is ultimately rooted in the supra-rational predisposition of the heart.

Rational beliefs form the main component of a worldview. These are beliefs that (1) objectively involve the most important, most fundamental matters in cosmic reality, and that (2) subjectively, although they certainly may be rational, are not open to scientific proof, or refutation, but are embraced with one's whole heart. There is a close relationship between one's rational beliefs and one's supra-rational faith. Those who adhere to certain beliefs without these being a matter of their hearts are like Christians who believe everything that is written in the creeds without being reborn. Conversely, those who "believe" without even a minimal ability to say *something* regarding *what* they believe have a faith that is void.

Faith itself is strictly supra-rational, and surpasses all formulations and confessions. But at the same time, adherents of particular worldviews can, to a certain extent, *express* their faith in rational formulations in which they account for their faith. These rational formulations are not their faith, but just the rational expression of it. Moreover, these formulations are always deficient and inadequate. But the faith of one's heart always surpasses all human insufficiency because it has been brought about by God's own Word and Spirit—or by the false gods.

"The" Western Worldview

We have seen that science can never be a neutral human activity but is always founded on certain presuppositions that are ultimately of a religious character. Mediating between a person's heart and his science is his worldview, which affects the foundations of his science and directs it in many ways.

I have to repeat again that the many specialists in science will hardly notice this. A specialist has been defined as someone who knows virtually everything about virtually nothing, whereas a generalist is someone who knows virtually nothing about virtually everything (this is written with tongue in cheek). You need the overview of the generalist to realize that science is rooted in the attitude of Western thinking in the broadest sense. This attitude is characterized by the strong (unprovable) belief that rational thinking is better than any form of non-rational thinking, the strong belief in the significance of empirical investigation, which includes the (unprovable) faith in the basic trustworthiness of our senses, the strong but indemonstrable rejection of solipsism and nihilism in science, the rejection of any form of appeal to the supernatural as a means of interpretation within science as such, etc.

These beliefs may sound self-evident, but you remember that for the critical philosopher nothing is self-evident. These are *beliefs*, very good beliefs—I hold them too—but they cannot be demonstrated beyond any reasonable doubt. The only (admittedly strong) evidence for their usefulness is the argument that science along these lines has been extremely successful. However, that statement does not affect the faith character of these beliefs.

We should never forget that this Western attitude, no matter how secularized it is at the moment, would have been unthinkable without the Judeo-Christian manner of thinking. Take for instance the empirical aspect of science. The ancient Greeks hardly cared about the empirical. They felt that our senses mainly deceive us, and that what reason worked out is always more reliable than what the senses could tell us. Aristotle was convinced that heavy things fell faster than lighter things because that was self-evident to him. With his reason, he "knew" this to be right. For many centuries, scientists believed this until Galileo proved Aristotle wrong by means of an *experiment*.

This was revolutionary: an *observation* refuted what had been self-evident to *reason* for almost two thousand years! What had brought Galileo and others to this new idea? Because the founders of modern science were Christians, they understood that they could not rationally *predict* how the Creator had necessarily put the world together. We call this the *contingency* of cosmic reality, which is the opposite of the alleged *necessity* of certain states of affairs. Allegedly, our reason can tell us *a priori* that they should necessarily be P. That is a mistake. The world is contingent: it could be P, but it could just as well be Q, or R, or S.

It is important for you to get this. Reason can never claim that the world *must* be P. Nobody can predict the way God reasons about the world. The only way to find out whether the world is P, Q, or R is to *interrogate* the world. We do this through investigation and experiment, that is, in an empirical way. In contrast to Aristotle, we do have confidence in our senses. We may *think* that the world must necessarily be P, but if our senses tell us it is Q, we accept the testimony of our senses. How do we know for sure that this is a better method than Aristotle's? We know it from the fact that in four hundred years science has made a thousand times more progress that in the two thousand years before that.

Of course, we do not leave reason aside, because reason has to make sense of our observations. But the basis for science is empirical in nature. Nobody besides some brilliant sixteenth-century Christians ever came up with this insight. I am not saying that nobody *could* ever have thought of it, but it simply did not happen. As long as Christian thinkers were still trapped in Greek thought, they did not find, and could hardly have found, the true basis for science. As soon as they freed themselves from Greek rationalism and anti-empiricism, as soon as they became modest *interrogators* of nature, they found this basis—and science became tremendously successful.

"Scientific" Worldviews

Modern secularized science works with borrowed premises. It owes its foundations to the early Christian thinkers but can no longer account for these foundations the way these early thinkers did. This is because contemporary scientists lack their worldview. Instead, we have seen that modern science has *absolutized* itself. That is, it has turned *science itself* into the worldview of modern Man, or rather, a number of different worldviews. Evolutionism (or Darwinism), capitalism, Freudianism, Marxism, materialism, humanism, and atheism have all become comprehensive worldviews that claim to be worthwhile because they are allegedly *thoroughly scientific.*

This is a disaster. First, they may appeal to science, but in themselves they are no more scientific than any "-ism" is. They are barely even philosophical; there are no philosophical schools named after the "-isms" just mentioned. They are just worldviews, sets of pre-scientific beliefs. Someone may assume that evolution has played a certain role in world history, but that hardly warrants evolution*ism*. People may believe that a free market is very important for our prosperity, but that hardly warrants capital*ism*. You may claim that suppression, defense mechanisms, and the like play a role in human functioning, but that hardly warrants Freudian*ism*. Matter is everywhere, but that does not mean that all is matter (material*ism*). God cannot be observed with our senses, but that hardly warrants athe*ism*, etc.

None of these "-isms" is scientific; they are worldviews at best and, to my mind, not very good worldviews at that. There is nothing wrong with worldviews *per se*, but do not try to sell them as scientific pictures of our world.

Naturalism

One of the most misleading of these scientific worldviews is *naturalism* as it has been preached recently by physicists like Stephen Hawking, Paul Davies, and Steven Weinberg. Such physicists identify physical reality with total reality. They suggest that if we understood all the properties of, and all relations between, subatomic particles, we would understand the whole of reality, including biotic and psychical life, human culture and religion. Davies claimed that "God is physics," and Hawking wrote that, when one day we have a (physical) Theory of All, we will know the mind of God.

Try to understand what is going on here. Of course, *a priori* there is not the slightest reason to assume that total reality is *limited* to what we can observe with our senses. Naturalism is not science; it is an "-ism," a worldview, that prefers to believe that there is nothing outside our empirical world. There is nothing scientific about it. Evidently, supernaturalism (the belief in an invisible world that transcends our empirical world) is no more scientific, or just as pre-scientific, as is naturalism. It is as much an "-ism," a worldview, that chooses to believe that there are things outside our empirical world. But at least, supernaturalists are not ashamed to admit that their conviction is a pre-scientific belief.

They do have a good argument, by the way, defending why they think their belief is to be preferred to naturalism. Their argument is that it would be an outright miracle if the world we can observe would exactly coincide with the world there is. Imagine, according to naturalism, that the whole world is a product of evolution, and our sense organs are too. What reason could there be to assume *a priori* that our sense organs precisely cover the entire world? It is an overestimation of the human senses as well as of human reason. I mean, there is no rational, and certainly no scientific, argument why naturalism is to be preferred to supernaturalism. The two are powerful worldviews, both with enormous consequences, but in the end precisely that—only worldviews. The choice between them is not determined by scientific arguments—how could that be?—nor even by rational arguments. They are rooted in the supra-rational, transcendent faiths of their respective adherents.

Consequences Within Science

These enormous consequences of both worldviews are not just religious. For instance, naturalism usually has great difficulty with parapsychology, the science of the paranormal (clairvoyance, telepathy, psychokinesis, and the like). That is because paranormal phenomena, as we know them so far, can hardly be fitted into physics, as we know it so far. Therefore—so the argument goes—they cannot exist. Whatever is not physics, is nothing at all.

Another example is offered by the French cell geneticist and Nobel prize winner, François Jacob, who rejected not only fundamentalist creationism, which rejects any form of evolution, but also orthodox (Neo-)Darwinism. He did so especially because of the inherent reductionism and absolutism of (Neo-)Darwinism, that is, its tendency to explain *all* reality, even society and culture, from the alleged process of evolution. The basic error is not only the strictly biological dubiousness of (Neo-)Darwinism as such, but also its false ideological presumption, that is, the confusion between evolutionary theory and evolutionism.

Similarly, the humanities pretend to offer explanations for the phenomenon of the human, but in reality they study only human corporeal existence, and then, only certain modal aspects of it. Nevertheless, many psychologists have claimed that their theories do actually address the essence of Man. Practitioners of depth psychology (Sigmund Freud, Alfred Adler, Carl G. Jung), behaviorism (B. F. Skinner, John B. Watson), and humanistic psychology (Abraham Maslow) each claimed in their own way to have penetrated into Man's innermost being. Today, psychology is much less presumptuous, but particularly in personality psychology, psychologists are still strongly led by worldviews. An example is a person's view concerning the contribution of *nature* (hereditary constitution) and *nurture* (education) to intelligence. In the United States, the Republicans lay more emphasis on nature, the Democrats on nurture. This has little to do with science, and a lot to do with their respective worldviews, which in turn affect their political views.

It will be understandable that the non-exact sciences, the humanities, are even more open to the influences of worldviews than the exact sciences. Here are just a few examples:

1. *Historical*: In the historical science, the underlying worldview determines whether one sees history as cyclical (e.g., Oswald Spengler, *The Decline of the West*) or as linear (e.g., the Christian view), whether one sees it as meaningful or meaningless (e.g., Theodor Lessing, *History As Giving Meaning to the Meaningless*), or whether one recognizes only immanent forces in history or also transcendent forces, etc.

2. Parts of *linguistics* are often plagued by the influence of Darwinism, which tends to belittle the difference between animal "language" and human language as much as it can. Over against this, linguists such as Noam Chomsky have suggested the existence of a *language acquisition device* (LAD), a module in the brain that accounts for the innate predisposition in young children to learn one or more languages. More recently, Chomsky exchanged LAD for the notion of "universal grammar" and the like. The exchange between classical Darwinism and these claims by Chomsky has more to with worldviews than with pure science.

3. *Social*: Every view of the social and societal aspects of life is dominated by the ongoing debate between liberalism, with its plea for *minimal* state power, and socialism, with its plea for *maximal* state power. Only in a few countries do we find functioning Christian political parties that endeavor to find a way between these two extremes, namely, *optimal* state power, guaranteeing the liberty of the individual, on the one hand, as well as caring for the weak, on the other hand.

4. *Economic*: The economic views that underlie capitalism and communism, as well as the many intermediate forms, varying from a free to a planned economy, are closely linked with the economists' worldviews. Karl Marx is *the* notorious example of the communist worldview, while the economic thinking of John Maynard Keynes cannot be severed from his liberalism, and that of Milton Friedman is rooted in his conservatism.

5. *Juridical*: Think of all the views regarding justice already mentioned in chapter 3. Is justice basically a biological matter (Social Darwinism), or a psychological matter (confusion of justice and sense of justice), a historical matter (product of historical development), or a social matter (justice is what 51% of the nation believes it to be), or is it an ethical matter (justice is to be governed by altruism)? Again, such questions have much to do with worldviews, and little to do with scholarship.

In summary, don't let anyone tell you that modern science is without prejudices, that is, ungoverned by worldviews! It is. And don't let anyone tell you that our (rational) worldviews are not governed by the ultimate (supra-rational) commitment of our hearts. They are. And if that is the case, there is no *a priori* reason why a Christian worldview would be worse than any other "-isms" in this world.

A Christian Worldview

In describing some features of a Christian worldview, I want to avoid too many theological considerations because this book is a philosophical introduction. Let us try to gain some access to a Christian worldview through our theory of the modal aspects.

1. *Logical*: A Christian worldview certainly has a rational, though not a theoretical, character. It is not rationalistic, however, because it assigns to the rational (or logical) its proper place among all the modal aspects of cosmic reality. In our Western world, the concept of truth has become very much a logical concept, whereas Christian philosophy emphasizes at least two other points. Firstly, truth contains many elements that are of a supra-rational, transcendent nature, especially the divine. Secondly, there is, for instance, also a social truth ("your conduct is asocial"), an economic truth ("this is of great value"), an aesthetic truth ("this is beautiful/ugly"), a juridical truth ("this is [not] righteous"), an ethical truth ("this is good/bad") and a pistical truth ("this is [not so] sure") (see the last chapter of this book). All these forms of truth are to be spoken of in a logically proper way—but that does not mean that they are *only* logical.

Moreover, our Christian worldview is *about* the logical, assigning to reason its proper modest place between so many other faculties of the human mind.

2. *Historical*: A Christian worldview is not a set of rigid beliefs, established once and for all. Christians will keep discussing their beliefs until the Second Coming of Christ. You may call yourself Reformed, for instance, but you would be amazed to find out how much your entire Reformed worldview differs from that of Reformed people in, say, the seventeenth century. I think there is far greater correspondence between (orthodox) Reformed people and Evangelicals today than between seventeenth- and twenty-first-century Reformed Christians! A Christian worldview, though confessing to be founded upon the Word of God, is constantly debated and refined in history—and sometimes it may fall into aberrations.

Moreover, the Christian worldview is a view *about* the historical, namely, a linear one: history is divinely meaningful in moving from creation to the "culmination of the ages," *via* the cross of Jesus Christ, and is driven by both human and transcendent forces.

3. *Lingual*: The wording of a Christian worldview is no slight matter. On the one hand, you want to remain as close to biblical parlance as possible but without falling into biblicism, which would mean quoting the Scriptures in such a way that they fit *a priori* into your own preconceived ideas. On the other hand, you would like to avoid non-biblical (which is not always a-biblical!) terminology as much as possible. This is difficult because we realize that we have imbibed thousands of modern non-biblical terms, which can hardly be avoided in the terminology of our worldview.

Moreover, our Christian worldview is *about* language. For instance, it emphasizes the significance of Scripture as Word of God, the Word of his mouth, the cosmic law-order as nothing else than the spoken *Word* of God for cosmic reality.

4. *Social*: Mistrust all Christians individuals, in your church, or on the Internet, who come up with some entirely new worldview of their own! That's not how worldviews arise. Worldviews are always the common property of whole communities. It is only together with all the Lord's saints that we can begin to grasp the

truth of God, and can attempt to incorparate it into some kind of Christian worldview (cf. Eph. 3:18). Sects are dominated by authoritarian leaders who allegedly have been specially called and inspired, allegedly have a special anointing, and who know it all. In church, we do things together. A Christian confession is the possession of the whole community. The Apostles' Creed is the common basis for almost two billion Christians in the world because, for them, it is both an ancient and an excellent summary of the essentials of their Christian faith. None of us has personally invented fire or the wheel; our worldview belongs to us all.

Moreover, a Christian worldview is a view *about* the social: about societal relationships in terms of creational ordinances, including marriage and family, church and state, etc.

5. *Economic*: In a Christian worldview, balance and equilibrium are very important. There must be no emphasis on human sinfulness at the expense of divine grace, or vice versa. No emphasis on divine sovereignty at the expense of human responsibility, and vice versa. No emphasis on the individual at the expense of the collective, and vice versa. No emphasis on Christ's divine nature at the expense of his human nature, and vice versa. No emphasis on internal Christian affairs at the expense of external relationships, and vice versa. No emphasis on theological knowledge at the expense of practical faith knowledge, and vice versa.

Moreover, a Christian worldview is *about* economics, for instance, about the biblical balance between the importance of personal property (contra communism) and putting a brake on landlordism (contra capitalism) (think of the biblical year of jubilee, in which all land reverted to its original owners; Lev. 25:8-55).

6. *Aesthetic:* Equally important is the harmony and beauty of a Christian worldview. It must be a sensitive and intellectual satisfaction to adhere to such a worldview. What pleasure could one find in solipsism and nihilism, in reductionism ("everything is nothing but this or that"), or even in materialism and atheism, except for the (irresponsible) simplifications that are inherent to them?

Moreover, a Christian worldview is *about* beauty. "Whatever is true, whatever is honorable, whatever is just, whatever is pure, whatever is lovely, whatever is commendable, if there is any excellence, if there is anything worthy of praise, think about these things" (Phil. 4:8).

7. *Juridical*: A vital element in a Christian worldview is the emphasis it lays on the meaning of the law-order of cosmic reality. God is the great Lawgiver. He has instituted his creational ordinances for the cosmos, and these laws guarantee order and regularity within created reality. God's law is the boundary between God and Man, that is, God is dependent on nothing, but creation is in all things dependent on him. God's law is the world order to which the ordered world is submitted. As the Lawgiver, God is elevated above his own laws, but creation, being below the boundary, is bound to them (see our extended discussion of this in chapter 4).

Besides, a Christian worldview is *about* righteousness. "For the is not a matter of eating and drinking but of righteousness and peace and joy in the Holy Spirit" (Rom. 14:17). As Jesus said: "But seek first the kingdom of God and his righteousness, and all these things will be added to you" (Matt. 6:33).

8. *Ethical*: What could be more important than the meaning of love within a Christian worldview? Try to figure out for yourself how love plays a vital role in all the different parts of your worldview! What is more characteristic of Christianity than (forgiving) love, both on God's side and on our side, both between God and Man, and among all human beings? Christianity is about serving God and the neighbor in the power of the love that has been poured out in regenerated hearts through the Holy Spirit (Rom. 5:5). "A new commandment I give to you, that you love one another: just as I have loved you, you also are to love one another" (John 13:34).

9. *Pistical*: Finally, the pistical aspect of a worldview expresses the thought that worldviews are sets of (rational, practical) *beliefs*, which are ultimately rooted in the (supra-rational, practical) *faith* of the human heart. A Christian worldview is a set of Christian beliefs, founded in the faith of the *regenerated* heart. "Now faith is the assurance of things hoped for, the conviction of things not seen" (Heb. 11:1).

To my mind, this is a striking conclusion: all science is based upon worldviews, and worldviews are ultimately rooted in love and faith—or the lack of them.

Questions for Review

1. Compare and contrast science, worldview, and faith.

2. Regarding a worldview, explain how the sensitive, logical, formative, social, and pistical aspects of a person's worldview operate.

3. Explain: "A worldview mediates between a person's heart and his science."

4. In what sense is it possible to say that every sane human has a worldview? In what sense might this be saying too much?

5. Why could and should a scientist not simply put his/her worldview aside when he/she does his/her scientific work?

6. Illustrate briefly how the following sciences are influenced by worldviews, including a Christian worldview:
    - historical science
    - linguistic science
    - social science
    - economic science
    - juridical science
    - ethical science

Chapter Nine
PHILOSOPHY AND THEOLOGY

Theological and Philosophical Guilt

A philosophy that wishes to be Christian can hardly avoid considering its relationship to theology. This is particularly the case because we live in a historical tradition in which theology has often claimed to be *the* representation of Christian faith. Both Christian philosophy and Christian theology are sciences, in the broad sense in which I have circumscribed this term before: forms of scholarship. But, remarkably enough, the relationships between philosophy and theology have always been rather strained, to say the least. In a famous lecture, the German philosopher Immanuel Kant spoke of "The Conflict of the Faculties" (1798), especially the conflict between the theological and the philosophical faculties. In my opinion, both theologians and philosophers were guilty of this conflict.

The theologians were guilty because (1) they often claimed that theology was the true Christian "philosophy"; (2) they asserted that they worked by the light of divine revelation, whereas, as they claimed, philosophy possessed only the light of human reason; and (3) they boasted that theology was capable of working out its own premises, and did not have, or need, any philosophical premises. I referred to these misunderstandings already in chapter 2. Moreover, theologians often confused theological and practical faith knowledge, elevated the former above the latter, submitted all science to theology as alone representing divine revelation, uncritically adopted pagan concepts and thought contents, or did all these things at once.

The philosophers were guilty because they claimed (1) that philosophy, that is, purely rational knowledge of reality, was the true "theology" (knowledge of God, or the gods, or the transcendent in general); (2) that working by the (alleged) light of divine revelation robbed theology of a truly scientific character, because only empirical observation and reason were to be accepted as sources of true knowledge; and (3) that the notion of a "Christian philosophy" was in conflict with the scientific demand for autonomy, neutrality and objectivity, and the rejection of all prejudices. See, again, chapter 2.

Some General Statements

Let us look at some of these allegations a bit more closely.

1. Theology is not "the true philosophy," and philosophy is not "the true theology." Although both may be Christian, they have very different callings and objectives, just like Christian psychology, Christian sociology, Christian ethics, etc.

2. Both Catholic and Protestant theologians have often claimed theology to be a supernatural, or sacred, science in contrast with other sciences because the former works by the light of divine revelation, whereas the latter have only the light of natural reason. This is a mistake. *All* sciences are occupied with divine revelation—although they may not recognize it—because God reveals himself not only in Scripture but also in nature, especially in the law-order for nature, which is his own spoken command for nature. God reveals himself even in cultural products because they too always presuppose the divine law-order. Science can be defined as the attempt to unveil the law-order that holds for reality, and in this law-order God reveals himself.

3. *All* sciences, including theology, work necessarily by the light of human reason because science is a logically qualified human activity. Even if many theologians claim to have a supernatural *starting point*, theological work as such is of a fully rational nature. In it, the theologian's logical faculty places itself over against the pistical modality of cosmic reality. In this respect, it differs essentially from practical faith knowledge, which is of a supra-rational, existential, transcendent nature.

4. Moreover, theology is as much an empirical science as any other science. It cannot make an academic investigation of God as such, in spite of its name: theology, that is, science about God (German: *Gottgelehrtheit*; Dutch: *godgeleerdheid*, "learnedness about God"). Strictly speaking, it can study only what people have said and written about God. Theologians study certain written sources, namely, the Bible and thousands of Jewish and Chris-

tian writings. Literary scientists do the same with literature, and historians do the same with historical sources that are relevant to them. In this sense, theology has sometimes been called a literary science, a set of theories concerning a specific type of literature, namely, Jewish and Christian literature, the Bible in particular. God cannot be laid on the dissection table of theological science, but writings about God can.

5. *All* science, including theology, has not only internal but also external, that is, philosophical, premises (often called *prolegomena*). They include the following: (a) Defining whether theology is a science depends on philosophical considerations concerning the differences between scientific and non-scientific knowledge. (b) The comparison between theology and other special sciences is founded on a philosophical totality view of cosmic reality. (c) Defining the study object of theology again presupposes a philosophical totality view of cosmic reality, in which this study object is delineated with respect to the study objects of other special sciences. (d) Defining the proper methodology of theology presupposes general criteria for scientific methodology, a topic that belongs to the subject matter of philosophy.

6. A Christian philosophy, or theology, is not *a priori* less scientific than a liberal, socialist, Darwinist, materialistic or atheist philosophy, or theology. The point that I have tried to make time and again in this book is that there is no such thing as a neutral, objective, unbiased science, whether philosophy, theology, or whatever science you may think of. Only specialists, people who oversee only a very small part of their own science, could live with the illusion of some neutral, objective science because they hardly ever touch upon the basics of their science. People with a much broader view will, I trust, understand what I mean much more clearly.

Philosophical Premises for Theology

Many of the philosophical errors that theologians have made in the past are the consequence of refusing to critically investigate the philosophical premises of their science. From a historical point of view, this is quite understandable when you look at the many harmful influences of *secular* philosophy, ancient or modern, within theology. However, the desire to get rid of all secular philosophy usually implies getting rid of philosophy entirely. The consequence is a lack of philosophical reflection upon the external prolegomena of theology. This leads to the inevitable result of theology falling into the very snare it wanted to avoid, that is, secular philosophy.

The reason is simple: theology cannot work without philosophical prolegomena. If it rejects the notion of a Christian philosophy, the first option involves ending up in the arms of ancient Scholasticism, that is, the semi-pagan philosophy of the Middle Ages and of early Protestantism. The second option is ending up in one of the modern or postmodern humanistic schools: (neo) positivism, existentialism, analytical philosophy, postmodernism, etc. The third option is landing in biblicistic fundamentalism, itself a bizarre mixture of Scholasticism and (neo)positivism of which fundamentalists themselves are unaware. Remarkably enough, both those who plead for a separation between theology and (Christian or secular) philosophy, and those who plead for a kind of interaction between theology and (secular!) philosophy, usually fall into one of these three snares.

In everyday practice, it turns out to be extremely hard to convey these things to the minds of theologians. I know this from experience because, apart from being a philosopher, I am a theologian myself. Great twentieth-century theologians, such as Heinrich Ott and Otto Weber, still spoke of theology and philosophy in terms of the relationship between revelation and reason—a false contrast, which I have refuted above. And Gerhard Ebeling said that "the orientation upon Jesus Christ" and the notion of sin are foreign to philosophy. Apparently, he was referring only to *secular* philosophy, without thinking of the possibility of a *Christian* philosophy. The semantic problems in the so-called "conflict between the faculties" are deeply rooted!

Of course, Christian philosophy does give a place to sin, to redemption, and to Christ. And it can do this without ever becoming theology because we must remember that theology does not have a monopoly on talking about God and the Bible. Christian philosophy, as well as every Christian special philosophy underlying one of the various special sciences, does talk about God and the Bible as well. Of course they do. From a Christian point of view, each and every one of the special sciences is rooted in a Christian worldview that refers to God and his Word.

Herman Dooyeweerd wrote in his *In the Twilight of Western Thought* (p. 142): "[I]f the possibility of a Christian philosophy is denied, one should also deny the possibility of a Christian theology in the sense of a science of the biblical doctrine. . . . Luther called natural reason a harlot which is blind, deaf, and dumb with respect to the truths revealed in the Word of God. But, if this prostitute can become a saint by its subjection to the Word of God, it is hardly to be understood why this wonder would only occur within the sphere of theological dogmatics. Why may not philosophical thought as well be ruled by the central motive of Holy Scripture?"

Dooyeweerd not only asked this question, but he also answered it by laying the foundations, together with Vollenhoven, for a Christian philosophy. Until today, however, unfortunately only a small group of orthodox theologians seem to have some idea of what such a philosophy might involve, and what its possible meaning might be for Christian theology. I refer to a philosophy that is no speculation, but is based on the solid ground of divine revelation. Already in 1955, the well-known German systematic theologian, Otto Weber, acknowledged the significance of a Christian notion of science, also for theology. He stated that such a Christian approach in fact existed, and referred to (in his time) recent attempts in the Netherlands to develop it. He quoted several works by Vollenhoven and Dooyeweerd. Other theologians did not refer to this philosophical school, but did—independently of it?—develop strongly related ideas. I mention in particular Emil Brunner, Paul Tillich, and Gustav Aulén, and to a lesser extent Paul Althaus, Helmut Thielicke, and Wolfgang Trillhaas.

Conversely, the Dutch philosopher and theologian, Andree Troost, saw in the theological conviction that philosophy is mere speculation the gateway to theology's own positivistic decline. A theology that wishes to be rooted in bare facts will in the end destroy itself because bare facts do not exist; there are only facts-for-people. I repeat: a theology that rejects Christian philosophy will inevitably land in some secular philosophy—often without realizing it—and that will be disastrous.

Rationalism versus Irrationalism

Let me give you a quite revealing example of what will happen if you refuse a Christian philosophical basis for your theology. This example involves the relationship between rationalism and irrationalism. Let me first point out that these are not theological but philosophical terms, and that they involve a strictly philosophical problem. No theological investigation as such can ever teach you what rationalism or irrationalism is, or the difference between them. Knowledge of such terms, and of their problems, belongs to your philosophical baggage, whether you realize it or not. If you are a theologian who refuses to study some necessary philosophy, you can hardly be aware of all the theoretical intricacies surrounding these terms. As a consequence, you can easily get lost. In Christian philosophy, the terms *rational* and *irrational* are carefully balanced against the terms *non-rational* and *supra-rational*. If you do not do that, the only alternative you can see for the rational and rationalism is the irrational and irrationalism.

An example of this is the theologian Millard J. Erickson. When his attempts to reconcile some difficult Scripture passages in an ingenious way are painted by opponents as forms of rationalism, Erickson answers that such criticisms are a consequence of the usual existentialist emphasis on the paradoxical nature of reality and the absurdity of the universe. You see what happens here? Erickson is—whether rightly or wrongly is not the point right now—accused of rationalism, and the only way he knows to answer this is by accusing his opponents of irrationalism. Apparently, he is not aware of the third and fourth options: the non-rational and the supra-rational. Other theologians did know about Christian philosophy's speaking of the supra-rational, but have rejected this as vague mysticism or metaphysical speculation.

In this way, traditional theology remains caught in rationalism because it knows no alternative, and this is because it has no philosophical framework in which the rational and the irrational, as well as the non-rational and the supra-rational, find their appropriate places. As long as theology works without a Christian philosophy that is concomitant with it, it will keep falling into the snare either of (Scholastic or Enlightenment) rationalism, or of ir-rationalist mysticism, or of biblicism.

Let me give you an example of the latter option. Many theo-logians are well aware of the snares of rationalist theology but think they are free from them. For instance, such a theologian may reply, "Also in this point Scripture will help me"—without realizing that Scripture as such does not supply us with instruc-tions as to how to avoid both rationalism and irrationalism. Scrip-ture does not even teach us how to do scientific theology at all.

Secondly, our theologian may say, "I simply adopt my doc-trines from Scripture, so nothing can go wrong"—without real-izing that Scripture as such does not offer any systematic treatise of any Christian doctrine. The theories of systematic theology are not adopted from Scripture but always designed by systematic theologians themselves. If done properly, it is done so as to ac-count for Scriptural data. But that does not alter the fact that the theories as such are the mental products of theologians. The Bible does not contain any theories, so you cannot draw theories from it. The fact is that theology never simply repeats what Scripture says but it is the product of human theological reflection upon Scripture, with all the beauties connected with such an enter-prise, but also all the perils, especially if you are not exactly aware of what you are doing.

Thirdly, our theologian may say, "The Holy Spirit will help me, and keep me from snares." Now, of course, this guidance of the Spirit is of eminent importance; as Jesus said, "When the Spir-it of truth comes, he will guide you into all the truth" (John 16:13). This holds for all believers, not just for theologians. But the theo-logian as such, who claims to do exegesis in a scientific way, has to realize that, if he does not account for his exegetical methodol-ogy, he will easily deceive himself. Such a theologian can easily confuse his own ideas with the work of the Spirit.

No Theology Without Philosophy

I hope I have shown at least that the problems involved are, by definition, *philosophical* problems, such as the relationship be-tween the rational and the irrational, or between faith knowledge and theological knowledge, or between heart and reason, or the problem of the so-called study object of theology, or of the pre-suppositions of theological hermeneutics (the science of interpretation), or the problem of theological methodology, in relation to, and in possible contrast with, the methodology of other special sciences, or the foundations of anthropology, or the problem of time and eternity, of immanence and transcendence, etc. The fact that, just as in other special sciences, these are *philosophical* problems implies that theology needs its own philosophical prolegomena, rooted in a coherent Christian cosmology and epistemology.

Of course, in many cases theologians in the past *did* realize the importance of philosophical prolegomena for theology. But usually they did not realize the importance of a *Christian* philosophy, that is, of philosophical prolegomena that are rooted in the same biblical ground-motive as theology itself. Usually, theologians who do see the importance of philosophy speak about it as if were some neutral enterprise, like the neutral tools of the carpenter or the physician. Such theologians freely quote either from ancient Scholasticism, or from modern pragmatism, existentialism, analytical philosophy, process philosophy, phenomenology, etc., without any bad conscience. But at the same time, they often remain strongly opposed to the notion of a *Christian* philosophy. This is quite a mystery, until one begins to realize the enormous power of Scholastic thinking, with its separation between theology and philosophy, and its denial of even the possibility of a truly Christian philosophy.

How can a truly Christian theology have such bad friends, or draw from such polluted waters? That is rather mysterious. Of course, I know very well that not everything in such secular philosophies is wrong. But where does the theologian find the *philosophical* help to know what he can responsibly adopt from these secular philosophies, and what not? Does he find it within his Christian intuition? Be wise, and mistrust it! Does he find it within his own theology? But theology was never equipped to answer philosophical problems. Why is the most obvious answer so unacceptable to many? They need a philosophy that has the same foundation as their Christian theology.

The Origin of Theology's Philosophical Premises

Nowadays many theologians have realized that they cannot do without philosophical presuppositions. The only remaining question is, *From where do they get them?* I see only three possible options:

1. *These philosophical prolegomena are derived from the Bible.* An example of this is the American theologian, Norman L. Geisler. He does accept a philosophical foundation for his hermeneutics, and finds it in theism, supernaturalism, and metaphysical realism. According to him, these "-isms" are taught, or at least presupposed, by Scripture. This is a theoreticalizing of Scripture, acting as if it taught, or even presupposed, any scientific or philosophical theory. Scripture neither contains nor presupposes theories or "-isms." Geisler does not seem to recognize the fundamental difference between the non-theoretical faith language of Scripture and the theoretical language of philosophy and theology. That is because he lacks a Christian philosophy in which such distinctions are analyzed.

2. *The necessary philosophical prolegomena are found in current philosophical tradition.* But what is this tradition? This is either medieval Scholasticism, which has survived until now in the bosom of traditional Roman Catholic and Protestant theology, or, during the last five centuries, in the humanistic tradition with its many ramifications. The correspondence between the two is that Scholasticism ties in with *ancient* (Greco-Roman) paganism, and humanism with *modern* paganism. Both are foreign to a theology that is rooted in the self-testimony of Scripture.

I repeat, this certainly does not mean that humanistic philosophy is useless to the Christian or to Christian theology. Firstly, every scientific enterprise, no matter how firmly it is grounded in an apostate ultimate commitment, contains important truth elements. The perspicuity of the truth shines through even the darkest philosophies. However, such truth elements are no excuse for also adopting the humanistic framework in which they are contained. Only a Christian philosophy can help us filter the truth elements from the rest of such philosophies.

Secondly, theology is never done on an island. It is always done over against, and in dialogue and interaction with, the culture to which it belongs, and thus also with the philosophical schools of its time. In that respect, the specific form of a certain philosophy or theology always has a limited significance, bound to the time in which it is designed. Thus, Dooyeweerd's philosophy was especially directed against one of the main philosophical snares of his own time, namely, Neo-Kantianism. Even the title of his main work, *A New Critique of Theoretical Thought*, ties in directly with Kant's main work, *Critique of Pure Reason* (i.e., Critique of Theoretical Thought). Today he would have chosen a very different title because the opponents are very different. Dooyeweerd's work has survived because it turned out to have great potential also in view of subsequent humanistic schools, including postmodernism. Philosophy and theology retain their relevance if they are capable of answering not only the questions of the time in which they were designed, but also the questions of later times. Such questions are often raised by secular philosophies. A Christian philosophy that is not relevant for a certain time period, including its secular philosophies, is useless.

3. The only option left is a philosophy that *is rooted in the same biblical ground-motive as theology itself,* and not in some Scholastic or humanistic philosophy. In the words of Gordon Spykman in his *Reformational Theology* (pp. 101-102): "Prolegomena must be of one piece with dogmatics proper. . . . Such integration is possible only if philosophical prolegomena and dogmatic theology are viewed as sharing a common footing. Though differentiated in function, prolegomena and dogmatics must be perspectivally unified. The major thesis at this point is therefore that the most fitting prolegomena to a Reformed dogmatics is a Christian philosophy. The noetic point of departure for both is Scripture. It provides the revelational pointers, the guidelines, the 'control beliefs' (Nicholas Wolterstorff) for shaping a biblically directed philosophy as well as a Christian theology."

Not so long ago, John D. Caputo argued that philosophy and theology, though different, are "companion ways" to nurture the "passion of life." This is what elevates Man above the boring stream of indifference and mediocrity, and what gives us something superlative to love more than we love ourselves. Though Caputo writes in a much more poetic way, it seems to me that this is not very different from what Dooyeweerd has called the ground-motive, and what others have called the ultimate commitment of thinking Man.

Misunderstandings

In this context, it is important to avoid three possible misunderstandings:

1. Of course, the choice of a particular Christian philosophy, or more specifically that of Dooyeweerd and Vollenhoven and their South African and North American companions, does not imply that a Christian theology is at all possible only *after* this choice. A radically Christian theology, and a Christian philosophy for that matter, is possible as soon as the—certainly not philosophical, nor theological—central ground-motive of the divine Word-revelation is really taken seriously. Time and again, theology has to find its starting point in this ground-motive, and not in ancient, Scholastic, or humanistic thought. If it does so, it will automatically (cf. *automatē*, "by itself," in Mark 4:28) move along Scriptural lines, and implicitly apply philosophical insights inspired by this ground-motive.

At the same time, it is obvious that theology will *gain* enormously from developing an explicit, coherent Christian philosophy, to underlie theology. Such a philosophy will constantly watch that in fact biblical, and not Scholastic or humanistic, ground-motives are introduced, and that theology will develop along the lines of the biblical ground-motive. The design of a Christian philosophy for theology will turn it from a naïve into a mature scientific theology.

2. It would be quite some misunderstanding to think that realizing the necessity of a radically Christian philosophy began only with Dooyeweerd and Vollenhoven, or with the one who greatly inspired them, Abraham Kuyper (1837–1920). On the contrary, this consciousness was never presumably entirely without adherents. Even before the Reformation, which certainly had some notion of it (John Calvin!), one could think of the thirteenth-century theologian and philosopher, Bonaventura. He spoke about *lumen cognitio-*

nis sensitivae, "the light of sensorily acquired knowledge," and *lumen cognitionis philosophiae,* "the light of philosophical knowledge," which form the underlying empirical and rational conditions for the respective sciences. Ultimately, he reduced these *lumina* to the one *lumen superius scripturae,* the "higher light of Scripture," and thus to the voice of Christ, the incarnate Word of God. In Bonaventura's view, apparently, both the special sciences and philosophy were to be rooted in God's Word-revelation.

3. The last misunderstanding to be mentioned is that, by choosing the approach of Dooyeweerd and Vollenhoven and their companions, we would greatly limit ourselves, and thus would hinder theological activity. In my opinion, this is not necessarily the case, because everything in this philosophy is open to criticism, improvement, replacement, and elaboration, except for two vital points. Firstly, the insight that a responsible theology must be rooted in external prolegomena, and these are, by definition, of a philosophical nature. Secondly, whatever philosophy the theologian may prefer, it must be one that is firmly rooted in the same biblical ground-motive as Christian theology itself.

Good and Bad Theology/Philosophy

Let me add here another necessary consideration. Is a radically Christian philosopher (or theologian) better than a Scholastic or humanistic philosopher (or theologian)? That depends on how you define "better." At this point, the distinction that Vollenhoven made between *structure* and *direction* can help us again. When it comes to the direction of the human heart, there are only two possibilities: directed toward God, or turned away from God. In this vertical sense, a radically Christian philosophy (or theology) is infinitely better than a Scholastic or humanist philosophy (or theology).

However, when it comes to the structure of philosophy (or theology), we think of the criteria for good, that is, academically expert, philosophy (or theology). Who is *academically* the better philosopher (or theologian)? In this horizontal respect, a Muslim or an atheist could be a successful philosopher (or theologian) if he correctly plays the "language game" of theology (to use Ludwig Wittgenstein's terminology), and correctly applies hermeneutical rules and theological methods. In short, this scientist obeys the rules implied in the structure of philosophy (or theology). Speaking strictly structurally, the good philosopher (or theologian) is the one who is academically outstanding. However, when it comes to direction, the Muslim or the atheist is doing *apostate* philosophy (or theology) because he works from an apostate ground-motive. Seen from this perspective, he is a bad philosopher (or theologian), and his achievements are definitely unsuccessful.

Every orthodox Christian theologian will readily admit that theology is to be rooted in a radically biblical ground-motive. Moreover, every truly academic theologian will recognize the need and presence of philosophical prolegomena in his discipline. Why, then, is it so difficult for many to see that the only philosophy that is to be used in the foundations of scientific theology is necessarily one that is rooted in the same radically biblical ground-motive? In terms of the vertical perspective, Muslim and atheist theologians are bad theologians. But is a Christian theologian who finds his external prolegomena in a philosophy that is rooted in a radically different ground-motive so much better?

Let me recapitulate. A consistent *humanistic* philosophy rejects both a Christian philosophy and a Christian theology, at least if this theology truly wants to be a scientific theology. A consistent *Scholastic* philosophy makes, as we have seen, a fundamental distinction between a neutral, objective, unbiased—therefore, certainly not Christian— philosophy on the one hand and sacred theology on the other hand. A philosophy rooted in the biblical ground-motive accepts both the possibility of a Christian philosophy and that of a scientific and yet truly Christian theology. If a Christian philosophy is not possible, then neither is a Christian theology. If a Christian theology is possible, then a Christian philosophy is possible as well. The humanists reject both. The Scholastic thinkers reject Christian philosophy, and accept Christian theology. As for us, we accept both, and even claim that you cannot have the latter without the former.

The Hermeneutical Circle

Here we have arrived at an interesting state of affairs. All arguments within Christian philosophy as to the possibility of a philosophy rooted in the biblical ground-motive are *a priori* to be explained from the biblical ground-motive of this Christian philosophy/theology. And all the denials of the possibility of a Christian philosophy/theology are ultimately rooted in the Scholastic or humanistic ground-motives of those who deny. We are dealing here with what is called a *hermeneutical circle* from which no thinker can escape. The theoretical question concerning the possibility or necessity of a Christian philosophy/theology is *a priori* determined by one's *pre-theoretical* ground-motive, which is either Christian or humanistic, or a Scholastic mixture of both. To put it in simpler terms: whether you believe in a (scientific) Christian philosophy/theology depends on how radical a Christian you are.

Do you realize what this means? In my view, the question whether you believe that all human thinking is rooted in a religious ground-motive depends . . . on your religious ground-motive. There is no way I could ever escape this conclusion. This is precisely what I meant when I spoke of the hermeneutical circle. If you do *not* believe that all human thinking is rooted in a religious ground-motive, I cannot help being convinced that this is because of *your* religious ground-motive. To put it a bit bluntly: your religious ground-motive forbids you to believe that human thought is always rooted in a certain religious ground-motive!

Let me try to illustrate this. Let us assume you are a rationalist, that is, you believe that human reason is the highest explanatory principle you know. You believe that everything you believe is to be based on logical arguments. My question to you is, how do you know this? How can you prove—that is, with the help of logic—that logic is the highest principle? In order to demonstrate that, you would need some higher mental position—the American philosopher, Hilary Putnam, has called it a "God's Eye point of view"— from where you can judge whether it is logical to be logical. If you could find such a position, it would be above logic, and thus you would refute your own viewpoint because what is above logic cannot be logical. The thesis, "It is scientific to assume that all fruitful ideas must be logical," is itself not logical, and thus apparently not scientific—the thesis refutes itself.

If you cannot find such a higher position, such a "God's Eye point of view," this means you cannot logically prove your position, so in that case your standpoint would be lost too. Apparently, you cannot be a consistent rationalist without refuting your own position. In other words, you too find yourself in a hermeneutical circle. You have to be a rationalist in order to believe that rationalism is such a good (logical) position.

As I have argued before, your choice of rationalism is in itself necessarily a *supra-rational* choice. In my terminology, it is a choice of the heart, and therefore in the end a decision of a religious character because it flows out of your ultimate commitment, the Ultimate Ground in which you put your confidence. So even if you are a rationalist, and you reject the notion of religious ground-motives, I think I can easily show not only that your position is untenable but also that your own thinking is rooted in a religious ground-motive. And as a Christian philosopher, I claim that in the end there are only two ultimate commitments: one that is congenial with the Word of God, and one that is not.

Foreign Elements in Christian Philosophy?

I have strongly emphasized that both philosophy and theology need to be of one piece, that is, they both need to be rooted in the biblical ground-motive. The question has come up whether that is not an illusion. Can an allegedly Christian philosophy, as well as a Christian theology, be truly only rooted in the biblical ground-motive? Let me give an example of this kind of criticism as it has been leveled against Christian philosophy. The Dutch philosopher, Theo de Boer, has asserted that Dooyeweerd has found his starting point in a Neo-Platonic theology. This claim holds water only if it can be shown that the correspondences that De Boer assumes between Neo-Platonism and Dooyeweerdian thought—if at all real, which I doubt—are *not* simply a consequence of a truth element within Neo-Platonism.

Such truth elements present themselves to us, and we can notice them without having any knowledge of previous philosophical schools that have noticed these very same truth elements. We meet with such truth elements in *all* philosophical schools because these schools—unconsciously—presuppose the revelation of God, no matter how they distort it. Therefore, if earlier philosophy P and later philosophy Q have Y in common, this does not necessarily mean either that Q has adopted Y from P, or that Q is a form or variety of P. Both could have arrived at Y independently.

The Dooyeweerd–Vollenhoven philosophy is nothing but a defective attempt to create a model of reality, so to speak. Of course, it cannot be *a priori* excluded that this attempt is partially or entirely governed at certain points by a secular (non-biblical) ground-motive. So far, I have never encountered convincing evidence of this. That means that, at present, I do not know of any philosophy that is of a more thoroughly Christian character than this one. It is not a perfect piece of human thinking—it is simply the only consistently Christian-philosophical cosmology I know.

At some point earlier, I mentioned the American philosopher, Nicholas Wolterstorff. He is a Christian, and a good philosopher. Some have considered him to be a serious rival to the Dooyeweerd–Vollenhoven school. However, his thought arises from a tradition that is founded upon a non-biblical ground-motive. The American philosopher, Hendrik Hart, has claimed that this non-biblical ground-motive also characterizes Wolterstorff's philosophical views. Therefore, I maintain my conclusion: at present, I know of no better philosophical starting-point for theology than the Dooyeweerd–Vollenhoven school.

Personally, I have discovered that this very extensive philosophy supplies us with answers in many subjects related to theology: the delineation of theology as such and of theology's study subject, the relationship between confession and theology, theological methodology, theological paradigms, and the principles of theological hermeneutics. More concretely, Christian philosophy helps to shape our opinions in many fields of theology itself. Christian-philosophical views of unity and diversity, constancy and variability, immanence and transcendence, structure and direction, concept and idea, modal and entitary structures etc. are of tremendous help. I know of no better tool that helps liberate theology from the claws of Scholasticism, biblicism and humanism. One day, I hope to show this more extensively in an *Introduction to Christian Theology*, which is going to be similar to the present *Introduction to Christian Philosophy*.

Questions for Review

1. In terms of the conflict between theologians and philosophers, in what ways has each side been guilty of making mistakes in thinking?

2. Explain what will happen if a Christian philosophical basis for theology is denied or ignored.

3. What are some philosophical problems inherent in doing theology?

4. What are three possible sources for the philosophical presuppositions of theology?

5. What are some of the possible misunderstandings about the relation between Christian theology and Christian philosophy?

6. Describe the nature and errors of a consistent humanistic philosophy and a consistent scholastic philosophy.

7. Why is it impossible to have a philosophy that is devoid of a religious heart-commitment?

8. Why, according to this chapter, is theology not a foundational science, like philosophy, but one of the many special sciences?

9. What is the difference between a theology of Christianity and a Christian theology?

10. If it is possible to speak of a Christian theology, would it be likewise possible to speak of, say, a Christian biology?

Chapter Ten

TRUTH

Every philosophy is interested in the question of truth. Some relativistic philosophers believe that there is no absolute truth, but even then they apparently show interest in the question as such. There is some difficulty in their point of view, though, because the statement, "There is no absolute truth," is itself presented as an absolute truth. Perhaps such philosophers should say something like this: "All truth is relative, this statement included." Other philosophers believe there is no absolute, all-encompassing truth, but perhaps only partial or relative truths.

Some postmodern philosophers believe that there *might* be some absolute truth, but that no philosophy or religion could ever demonstrate beyond doubt that it possesses the truth. Even if there were some absolute truth, we would have no way of knowing it. If it were otherwise, we would all have found the truth long ago. Instead, numerous religions, ideologies, and philosophies that are irreconcilably different claim to have the truth. Because there are so many of them, we can safely conclude that *none* of them has the truth–or so these philosophers believe.

Do not say that postmodern philosophers believe in the absolute truth of their own position, because that may sound ingenious, but it is factually wrong. Plato, who said of the Skeptics: "Skeptics are skeptical about everything except about skepticism," may have been right. But it does not hold for postmodernists because postmodernists relativize all positions, including their own.

Other philosophers believe there is an absolute truth, and that their approach is the best way to find it, or they even claim to possess it. Like every religion and every ideology, so too every philosophy has to take a standpoint on this matter. What, for heaven's sake, can Christian philosophers add to this massive confusion?

Is Christian Philosophy True?

Of course, Christian philosophy takes great interest in truth, too. But watch out: it is one thing to state, as a *believer*, that Jesus Christ is the Way, the Truth and the Life (John 14:6), or that "Your Word is truth" (John 17:17), or to confess that "the truth is in Jesus" (Eph. 4:21). But that does not necessarily mean that our Christian *philosophy* is truth! We may have a perfect starting point of faith on the supra-rational, transcendent level, but that does not automatically yield a perfect philosophy on the rational, immanent level. You may be "on the side of truth" (cf. John 18:37), or be "of the truth" (1 John 3:19), but that does not mean that everything *you* produce is truth.

In the previous chapter, we saw that the phrase *true science*, or *true philosophy*, is ambiguous. On the one hand, we have to distinguish between genuine science, that is, science done in obedience to the cosmic law-order, and pseudo-science, that is, science in which these structural laws are disobeyed or ignored. I am referring to the structural laws for science that are anchored in the divine law-order. On the other hand, we distinguish between true science, that is, science oriented towards the Creator, and false science, that is, science of an apostate nature. If there is any truth in science at all (see below), we expect to find it above all in science that is both genuine (i.e., of high academic quality) and truthful (directed towards the Truth).

Before we move on, let us look a bit more closely at the term *truth* as such. In the first place, truth is an ontological term. It refers to the "really-being-so" of reality, or of a certain field of investigation. "The sky is blue" is an ontological statement, which truthfully refers to the blueness of the sky. Truth is also an epistemological term: knowledge can be described as possessed truth. "I know the sky is blue" is an epistemological statement, meaning, "I possess the truth concerning the blueness of the sky."

This is quite an elementary approach to the notion of truth. It is the truth that also occurs in the Bible, as well as in everyday life. This or that is true if and only if it is really the case. "Is it true you went to school today?" "Yes, that is true." "That is really the case."

However, the notion of truth is frequently dealt with on a more profound level in the Bible, namely, as trustworthiness (please note that in English, *truth* and *trust* are etymologically from the same root). This is the meaning of the Hebrew term ʾĕ *met*, which means both *truth* and *faithfulness*, with the collateral meaning of *trustworthiness*. God is truth in that he is absolutely trustworthy in all he says and does, and worthy of our unconditional *trust* (confidence) and loyalty (Ps. 31:5; Jer. 10:10; Rom. 3:4, 7). That is the same as saying that God is *faithful* in all he says and does, and thus worthy of our confidence.

Man, too, is to be truth; truthful men are reliable, trustworthy men (Exod. 18:21; cf. Neh. 7:2). When we compare various translations of the Old Testament, we will see that often some translations have "truth(ful)," where others have "faithful(ness)." A "man of truth" is a faithful, trustworthy person, and is such primarily in the eyes of God. God is "truth" (faithful, trustworthy) toward Man, Man is "truth" (faithful, trustworthy) toward God as well as his fellow men. "A faithful [or truthful, trustworthy] man who can find?" (Prov. 20:6b).

In summary, in the Bible *truth* refers either to truth in its practical *immanent* meaning of (knowledge about) the "really-being-so" of immanent things, or to truth in its practical transcendent meaning as referring to the transcendent-religious relationship between God and Man, that is, the "really-being-so" of transcendent things. In both cases, we have to do with a *practical* notion of truth, not a *theoretical* one. Within philosophy and the special sciences, we are especially interested in theoretical truth. Practical truth and theoretical truth have to be carefully distinguished: the Bible is true, but a Christian philosophical or theological theory, though intended to be faithful to the Bible, may very well be false. Let us investigate this matter a little more closely.

Science and Truth

Can philosophical and scientific theories—including theological theories—ever be truth at all? I believe they can, although only to a certain extent. Science can be an approximation of the truth (the really-being-so) of a certain field of investigation, no matter in how limited a way. But this answer has to be qualified. On the one hand, there is the danger of logical positivism, which is *too optimistic*. It claims to start with objective facts about cosmic reality, which are then allegedly represented in scientific theories. Also theologians often—usually unconsciously—take this positivistic approach. They believe that their theories represent a certain part of (biblical/ Christian) reality, or even that their theories are "drawn" from (biblical/Christian) reality. This is a rather naïve kind of philosophy or theology, in which scientific truth is highly overestimated.

On the other hand, there is a biblicistic negativism, which is *too pessimistic*. This is the view that scientific theories are only useful instruments to help us in finding our way within cosmic reality, but that truth is only to be found in Scripture. No truth outside the Bible! Such an attitude, which is factually anti-scientific and obscurantist, overestimates God's Word-revelation at the expense of his creational revelation. In other words, they forget that not only Scripture, but also God's revelation in the creational cosmic reality, contain truth. And because this is *God's* revelation in nature, we definitely have to do with *God's* truth here. The American philosopher, Arthur F. Holmes, has expressed this in the title of a book, *All Truth Is God's Truth*. All things that are true, in some way or another are divine truth, for they can be true only in the light of the law-order that God has instituted for cosmic reality. I will further explain this below.

All science aims at unveiling this truth of God as it is enclosed in God's creational revelation, with two restrictions: (1) most philosophers and scientists do not accept that science essentially deals with *God's* truth, and (2) in practice, science can approximate this divine truth only in a defective and preliminary way. Science searches for the divine law-order of cosmic reality, but in practice our theoretical formulations of these laws are at best vague, and often constantly varying, approximations of this law-order. However, that does not deny the fact that they are approximations of divine truth, as the latter is disclosed by science.

God Teaches the Farmer

God brings truth to light not only through the Bible, but also through Man's cultural task. This is beautifully illustrated by Isaiah 28:24-26: "Does he who plows for sowing plow continually?

Does he continually open and harrow his ground? When he has leveled its surface, does he not scatter dill, sow cumin, and put in wheat in rows and barley in its proper place, and emmer as the border? For he is rightly instructed; his God teaches him."

Here we see that it is God who instructs the farmer as to how he has to work his land (culture!), but in practice the farmer learns this by paying attention to the natural laws—which are *divine* laws—manifesting themselves in every crop. The farmer learns from the Lawgiver by giving heed to his law-order. This is the way in which the scientist also learns from God. True science is not necessarily knowledge that is explicitly found in Scripture, but it is science founded on a proper scientific methodology, and in a Christian worldview.

Another biblical example is found in Genesis 2:19-20: "Now out of the ground the LORD God had formed every beast of the field and every bird of the heavens and brought them to the man to see what he would call them. And whatever the man called every living creature, that was its name. The man gave names to all livestock and to the birds of the heavens and to every beast of the field."

In the Bible, the name expresses the essence of that which is named. So God's question to Man entails that he should penetrate into the essence of the things that God had created. This is closely related to what science is doing. In naming the animals, Man was bound to the animals' objective characteristics; he could not call an earthworm a winged animal, or a jellyfish a vertebrate. But the names themselves were his creation, his design. Please note that God brought the animals to Man "to see what he would call them." Apparently, that was not determined in advance. Humanly speaking, God was curious about what Adam was going to do.

In this naming of the animals there was an objective element—giving heed to their properties—but also a subjective element; that is, each name expressed not only something of the animal, but also something of Man himself. It is the same in science. On the one hand, scientists have to do justice to the "really-being-so" of the things they investigate. On the other hand, there is a strongly creative or inventive element in every scientific theory. As the great Austrian philosopher of science, Karl Popper, has expressed it, the facts are *discovered* (that is the objective part), but the theories are *designed,* or *invented,* to account for the facts (that is the subjective part). Theories are free creations of the human mind.

Theories of Truth

In everyday life it seems so simple: a statement is true if and when it corresponds with reality. However, in philosophy nothing is self-evident, as I have mentioned before. The circumscription I just gave you has been called the *correspondence the*ory. In everyday life this theory is self-evident: if my eyes see a ditch before my feet, I would not be able to function if I could not trust my eyes that there really is a ditch before my feet. What is, I see; what I see, is. So far, so good. However, you have to realize that *as a philosophical theory*, it is not good enough. The great problem with it is that we have no way to check it. For our everyday experience, that is no hindrance. We neither need nor demand proofs for the thesis that a statement is true if and when it corresponds with reality; for practical thought, this is not even a thesis or a theory. In theoretical thought, however, we seek evidence. But again, we have no "God's Eye point of view" from where we can compare our statements with reality. Therefore, *as a theory*, the correspondence *theory* is in trouble. It is too audacious.

Let us apply these considerations to scientific theories. We might say that theory P is true if and when it corresponds with reality. But the only things we have are our sense data. We observe reality, especially small realities imitated in the laboratory, and on the basis of the sense data we have obtained we create an explanatory theory. But how do we know that it corresponds with reality? Let us assume that, so far, no data have become known that are in conflict with P. But what does this prove? Perhaps some theories Q, R, and S are conceivable that would explain the data equally well, or even better. The only thing is that, so far, we could not think of another theory; we are glad we found one at all. But Q, R, and S remain theoretical options! At any rate, we cannot claim that P represents the *truth* about the study object concerned. How could we ever know?

For this reason, several more modest theories of truth have been invented. The *coherence theory* says, "A statement is true if and when it is coherent, or consistent, with the other statements within a certain system of thought." Truth is not found in distinct statements but in the continuous adding of statements to a system. Truth "is" not but gradually "becomes" as the system is growing and keeps being refined.

The *pragmatic theory* is even more modest: a statement is true if and when it works, when it proves to be useful. In theology this would mean, "If the 'God hypothesis' works satisfactorily, it is true." But what if such a hypothesis turns out to work for some persons, and not for others? It is then both true and false? This seems to be a valid objection, but pragmatic thinkers will not be impressed. They will simply answer: We have nothing better, so we will have to live with it. Think of what I just said about theory P. The best we could say is that it works fine—although Q, R, and S might have worked fine too—so for the time being we accept P as true. In fact, this is the attitude most scientists are taking all the time with regard to their theories. They are true as long as the scientists concerned do not have anything better.

There are several other theories of truth—the performative theory, the existentialist theory, the redundancy theory, the consensus theory—but I have to leave them aside at this point.

Correspondence

The only theories that I will discuss a bit further are the correspondence theory and the coherence theory. Do not underestimate the latter! It plays a definite role in all theory building because—in theology, for instance—statements not only should not contradict the Bible but should not contradict one another either. The coherence theory is of great importance *within* a certain thought system. But in the end, we will always want to know how our philosophical models and scientific theories relate to the "really-being-so" of reality, that is, *to the truth about reality.*

The correspondence theory seems to be what we are looking for, but I mentioned to you already that what seems to be self-evident in everyday thinking, philosophically speaking has no leg to stand upon. Its starting point is that there is an external, objective (i.e., observation-independent) reality, but it forgets that, *as a theory*, it has no independent access to that reality to check if our scientific theories correspond with it. The certainty it has concerning objective reality is not contained in any philosophical *theory* at all, but is a supra-rational and supra-empirical confidence of the believing heart. Such a heart possesses a very strong argument: a heart that has placed its trust in God cannot accept that that same God would present our senses—which he has created himself—with the image of a cosmos that in reality did not exist.

This confidence is not a correspondence theory, nor any other theory. It neither needs, nor desires a theory, but it is beyond theories. Do not think this is just playing with words! If you would turn the supra-theoretical confidence of our hearts into a theory, this would just be evidence of the enormous power of the theoreticalizing of life, that is, of the tremendous power of rationalism and scientism in our culture.

I repeat, the fact that there is some external reality is not the outcome of any philosophical thinking, but is a pre-philosophical, pre-theoretical confidence of the heart. We believe in an external reality not because the correspondence theory teaches it, but because we believe in God. If Norman L. Geisler asserts that the correspondence theory is indirectly taught by the Bible, I understand what he is trying to say, but he confuses practical and theoretical thought. The Bible teaches no theories, neither directly nor indirectly. What Geisler wants to say is nothing more than that the person who believes in God also believes that there is some world he has created, and that through our senses we have empirical access to this world. This has nothing to do with any theories whatsoever, as Geisler should have realized. Bringing in the word *theory* suggests an overestimation of theoretical thought. No wonder that such things happen: this overestimation has been going on for more than twenty-three centuries.

Scientific Realism

The view that philosophical and scientific theories, no matter how defective and preliminary, are approximations of cosmic reality is called (scientific) *realism*. The view that scientific theories are just useful, convenient instruments, which do not tell us anything about what reality really is, is called *instrumentalism*. Plato has been called the father of the former, Aristotle the father of the latter view. When the revolutionary work of Copernicus on the movements of the celestial bodies appeared in 1543, the Lutheran theologian, Andreas Osiander, wrote a foreword. He claimed that Copernicus' theories had to be taken—in our terminology—in an instrumentalist sense; that is, they said nothing about how our solar system really worked. In order to understand this subject, one had to turn to the Bible.

Cardinal Roberto Bellarmine, too, would not have condemned Galileo Galilei for his heliocentric views if the latter had only taken his theories in an instrumentalist sense. However, Galileo interpreted them in a fully realistic way, and so the Roman Catholic Church felt it had to condemn him (1633). By the way, this was not so much because Galileo contradicted the Bible—as people have asserted—but because he contradicted Aristotle.

Another thinker, the eighteenth-century British bishop, theologian, and philosopher, George Berkeley, strongly defended an instrumentalist view with respect to Isaac Newton's theory of gravity. A realistic view seemed to entail that this theory revealed truth about physical reality through the force of the intellect, without the help of divine revelation. Berkeley was afraid that such a realism would pose a great threat to faith and to the authority of the Bible. According to him, Newton's theory was only a mathematical hypothesis, that is, a useful instrument to calculate certain phenomena, but not a true description of something real.

The interesting question one might ask at this point is whether these theologians, Osiander, Bellarmine, and Berkeley, and many theologians after them, would have been prepared to take an instrumentalist standpoint with respect to theological theories as well! Why should one be an instrumentalist when it comes to natural scientific theories, and a realist when it comes to theological theories? The only reason for this would be Scholastic prejudice: the alleged dualism between *grace*, to which sacred theology belongs, based upon God's Word-revelation, and *nature*, to which profane (secular) philosophy and the other sciences belong, based upon the light of natural reason only.

Instrumentalism

In the nineteenth century, Christian scientists like Michael Faraday, James Clerk Maxwell, or Louis Pasteur, would have had no difficulty assuming that science throws light on God's creational ordinances. In the twentieth century, this changed drastically, especially when Albert Einstein in principle overthrew Newtonian physics. This was dramatic because many nineteenth-century physicists had considered it to be necessary truth. The confidence of scientists with regard to such a reliable science as physics was deeply shaken. The situation was also worsened by philosophical developments, such as the rise of radical historicism, pessimistic philosophies (especially Arthur Schopenhauer and Friedrich Nietzsche), psychoanalysis (Sigmund Freud, Alfred Adler, Carl G. Jung), vitalism (particularly Henri Bergson), and existentialism (especially Martin Heidegger and Jean-Paul Sartre). As a consequence of all these developments, scientists tended to move from realism to the more reticent viewpoint of instrumentalism.

As someone wrote at that time: "Theories are to reality, not as soup is to soup meat, but as a wardrobe number is to a coat." That is, theories are not drawn from reality as soup is drawn from soup meat. They are rather like coat check numbers: handy for finding your coat, but telling us nothing about what the coat looks like.

However, instrumentalism, too, met with strong objections. First, this viewpoint cannot explain the fact that theories can give rise to risky predictions, which moreover often come true. If theories are only theoretical fictions, how can one explain that they can even lead to the discovery of wholly new phenomena? Thus, on the basis of the planets' movements, the existence and location of a new planet was predicted, which was indeed discovered. It received the name Neptune.

Second, how can one explain that certain theoretical fictions, such as Kekulé's discovery of the ring structure of certain molecules (e.g., benzene), today can be made visible in an almost direct way with the help of an electron microscope?

Third, how can instrumentalism explain the tremendous success of technology, if the physical theories on which the latter is based in some way or another would have nothing to do with the "really-being-so" of nature?

Critical Realism

The objections against instrumentalism did not lead to a return to the old realism, which had turned out to be too naïve. It was clear by now that theories are not simply copies, images, representations of reality. If that were the case, how could one explain that no single theory has a permanent character, but that all theories, even the best established, in the long run are replaced, or at any rate fundamentally modified? At least *something* had to be learned from instrumentalism, which had claimed that, for every set of observational data, in principle a large—perhaps even an infinite—number of theories is conceivable. I mentioned this point before. It may be difficult to find one single theory to explain the observations, but that does not mean it is the right theory. At best, it is one good theory out of many potential good theories. They are good, not because they reflect reality, but because they involve a meaningful and consistent interpretation of the observational data *and* allow for a further testing of this interpretation. However, in principle numerous other meaningful, consistent and testable interpretations are always conceivable, and even probable.

Let us assume that, out of numerous possible theories, we had chosen the right one, that is, the one representing reality correctly. In that case we could never *know* that we had found the right one. This is because, again, we have no "God's Eye point of view" from where we can compare our theories with reality. The only thing we *can* know is that a certain theory has turned out to be a wrong one because too many newer observational data no longer fit into the theory. Subsequently, a new theory has to be designed that is capable of interpreting both the older and the newer data in a meaningful coherence.

If we succeed, so much the better. But also with regard to the new theory we have to state that we can never know whether it is the right one because, in the end—it may take years or centuries—the new theory will also become obsolete because of newer observational data. What I said before remains valid: in principle for every set of data an infinite number of theories is conceivable—even if we are thankful for having found at least one.

The newer, so-called "critical" or "qualified" realism combines the insights of the old realism (theories have "something" to do with reality) and instrumentalism (theories can never be called representations of reality). It is the view that theories cannot be "drawn" (adopted) from reality as such, but are designed by scientists to explain the observational data. This realism maintains, however, that theories which fulfill academic criteria indeed have to do, no matter in what restricted sense, with the "really-being-so" of reality.

It is true that the formulations of scientific laws are invented; in this respect, critical realism agrees with instrumentalism. But the lawful coherences themselves are discovered, as the old realism claimed. In effect, theories *are* instruments, but then, instruments to get closer to the truth concerning the field of investigation. We may truly claim again that scientists are definitely occupied with creatively mapping out the law structures of cosmic reality. Science is not copying reality (*contra* realism), but it is no order-creating activity either (*contra* instrumentalism): it is an order-*disclosing* activity. In Christian philosophy, *order* refers to the law-order that the Creator has instituted for the cosmos.

Of course, also within critical realism there are different opinions. Some argue that we should be satisfied with the coherence theory (see above) as being the best we can get. Others want to limit themselves to trying to understand theories from their historical developments. This does not necessarily mean that such realists are not interested in some observation-independent reality, or in truth, but only that they are conscious of their own limitations. That is, if you want to *know* that observation-independent reality, design theories as well as you can. These are theories that cover the observational data and have high predictive value, and thus constantly inspire scientists to ever further investigations. In continuing to do so, we may safely say that, in the end, we will be closer to the truth about our field of investigation than we were before. Whether you are sure about that, or more hesitant, depends very much on your worldview.

Theoretical Truth

At this point, we come to an important insight. Even if we could be absolutely sure—which we cannot—that a certain theory is right, i.e., that it is *the* correct representation of a certain field of investigation, what kind of truth would it contain? It would only be some *theoretical* truth, that is, truth obtained through modal abstraction, which is by definition *partial* truth. Knowledge of the truth, properly speaking, is never obtained in theoretical (i.e., abstract, detached, one-sided) thought, but only in practical (i.e., concrete, immediate, integral) thought. Only in this way is it possible to grasp the nature and meaning of cosmic reality in its fullness and unity, and in its transcendent orientation toward the Creator.

Take a simple example. If you have learned that water is actually H_2O, can you now say you know what water really is? I do not think so. You now know only something of the physical aspect of water. But to the full reality of water also belongs the fact that water is basic to all living organisms (biotic aspect), that water can refresh you, that water can wash you, that water can threaten you, that water can gladden you (think of the beauty of a waterfall, or of the ocean; aesthetic aspect), that water can be a symbol of the Holy Spirit (John 7:38-39; pistical aspect), etc. In Christian philosophy, the full reality of water, which is far more than any single aspect can express, includes at least all its object-functions.

This practical way of dealing with the full reality of things is the one we encounter, for instance, in Job 38-41, where Man stands in relation to creation by the light of God's Word. This practical thinking and knowing is definitely not simple, childish, or naïve. On the contrary, the profoundest knowledge we have of cosmic reality is of a supra-rational, transcendent nature, and is founded on God's Word-revelation. This faith knowledge far surpasses our (alleged) scientific knowledge of creation. The reason is that this faith knowledge leads us to Christ, who is the Truth (John 14:6), in the power of the Holy Spirit, who is the "Spirit of truth" (John 14:17; 15:26; 16:13). In, through, and for Christ, all things have been created (Col. 1:16). Christ is the One "in whom are hidden all the treasures of wisdom and knowledge" (Col. 2:3).

Over against "philosophy and empty deceit, according to human tradition, according to the elemental spirits of the world" (Col. 2:8), the apostle Paul does not place some Christian philosophy, but more than that: Christ himself. Christian philosophy finds its meaning in him to whom it points, Christ, whereas "hollow and deceptive philosophy" leads away from him. Christian philosophy is always defective and preliminary; therefore it can never be called truth—but its starting point and purpose are the Truth. Secular philosophy may contain important and valuable truth elements, that are worth filtering out—but it is not founded on the Truth, and in the end leads away from the Truth. The truth elements in secular philosophy can be disclosed only by being referred back to practical faith experience, which is oriented toward the full Truth by the light of God's Word and Spirit.

Biblical experiencing and thinking is pre-theoretical, or if you like, supra-theoretical, but definitely not naïve, in the sense of childish innocence and limited understanding. Secular philosophy of science has often called everyday practical thinking naïve because of a tremendous overestimation of scientific thinking and knowing (recall what I said earlier about scientism). However, in a sense, it is rather the non-biblical experiencing and thinking that may be called naïve because it is dominated by apostate thinking. In its primitive form, this thinking may be fraught with mythical elements, as was still the case with almost all ancient thinkers. But even in the most highly developed form of this thinking, apostate Man remains closed to the light of the divine revelation. As a consequence, his thinking remains enclosed within his own experience, which he, moreover, views in the wrong transcendent perspective.

Again we see here how practical thinking may far surpass theoretical thinking, namely, there where biblical (supra-theoretical) thinking stands over against apostate (theoretical or supra-theoretical) thinking. This does not mean that biblical thinking also could not partially fall into the grip of apostate thinking under the influence of sin. Only if and when the Christian consciously opens his heart to the fullness of the Truth that is in Christ, and that is revealed to us in Scripture, will the light of eternity shine over all dimensions of experiential reality. Then, the Christian will see all things as they really are, in the light of the creational order that God has instituted for cosmic reality, and that is anchored in Christ, in whom they were created, and in whom they will one day find their fulfillment.

Partial Truth

It is Christian philosophy that has pointed out that theoretical truth can never be the full—integral, absolute, all-sided—truth for at least three reasons:

1. Theoretical truth is specialized truth in that it refers to only one specialized, abstracted modal aspect of our full, practical experience of reality. Thus, biological knowledge refers only to the biotic aspect, juridical knowledge only to the juridical aspect, theological knowledge only to the pistical aspect of truth. Even theological truth is, as theoretical truth, necessarily one-sided, detached, abstracted knowledge, and thus never identical with the full, practical faith knowledge of the heart.

2. Theoretical truth is at best intended truth: the intended correspondence between science and reality is only approximated. I repeat, we have no independent means to establish whether the intended correspondence has ever been reached. Therefore, we call scientific theories good, not because of some alleged correspondence, but because of (a) the internal coherence and consistency of the logical argumentation, (b) the ever greater refinement of their internal structure, (c) the efficient theoretical entities within them, and (d) the metaphors used in them, which are continually fertile and capable of ever further extension of the theories involved.

3. Theoretical truth is truth that by definition refers to what is logically correct or incorrect, and in this respect is only partial truth as well. The reason is that in practical experience there are many other, non-theoretical truth experiences, such as:

(a) *Social* truth, in which social conduct is true, and asocial conduct is false—not logically false, but socially false.

(b) *Economic* truth, in which the valuable stands over against the worthless. Of course, economics as a science is a logically qualified enterprise, but "the economic," as the kernel of the economic modality, has to do with balance and value. In the economic sense, value is not a matter of logic, but of the market. The market has its own truth, which cannot be reduced to the logical.

(c) *Aesthetic* truth, in which the harmonious and the beautiful stand over against the disharmonious and the ugly. Aesthetic judgments have their own truth, which, again, cannot be reduced to the logical. This or that is beautiful, not on the basis of rational arguments but of aesthetic criteria. We can logically *argue* about these criteria, as is done within the science of aesthetics, but "the aesthetic" as such is not logical; it is something entirely unique.

(d) *Juridical* truth, in which justice (that which is righteous) stands over against injustice (that which is unrighteous). This is neither a purely sensitive, nor a purely logical matter, although juridical acts also function in the sensitive and the logical aspect. The juridical is something unique.

(e) *Moral* truth, which is concerned with what is good, moral, ethically correct, over against what is bad, evil, immoral, ethically incorrect. Again, this is neither a purely sensitive, nor a purely logical matter, although moral acts also function in the sensitive and the logical aspect. The ethical is something unique.

(f) *Pistical* truth, which is concerned with that which is sure, reliable, worth placing your confidence in, over against that which is uncertain, unreliable, not worth placing your confidence in.

It is important to understand this correctly. If it is true that this or that is good or beautiful, it is never a particular science that determines this. Science is concerned only with what is logically correct or incorrect. Ethics investigates rationally *why* people call this or that good, and tries to formulate ethical criteria. It can logically argue about such criteria, but it can never *reduce* the ethical as such to the logical. Aesthetics investigates *why* people call this or that beautiful, and tries in a logical way to formulate aesthetic criteria. But it can never reduce the aesthetic as such to the logical. It is Man who, in his practical knowing-attitude, distinguishes the good, or the beautiful, or the righteous, or the valuable things.

Every science that is no longer strictly descriptive but becomes prescriptive, leaves the field of strict science, and enters the field of worldviews. Theology is again an excellent example. As a special science, strictly speaking it involves only the logical correctness or incorrectness of theological theories. Only in his supra-theoretical faith knowledge does the believing theologian refer his theoretical knowledge to the faith truth that is in Christ.

The a priori *Elements of Truth*

Before I come to my last topic, let me briefly explain the difference between *transcendental* and *transcendent*. Transcendental has to do with the ultimate grounds or conditions of all knowledge. Transcendent refers to anything that surpasses our immanent reality. The transcendental *a priori* of all true knowledge is, on the one hand, the recognition of the structural laws that God has instituted for cosmic reality, and on the other hand, the recognition of the structural laws for the true attainment of knowledge concerning cosmic reality. The first one is an ontological *a priori*, the second one an epistemological *a priori*. They possess an *a priori* character in the sense that the structural laws both for reality and for knowledge, which are both contained in the cosmic law-order, are pre-given by God, that is, precede all attainment of knowledge.

In summary, the cosmic law-order is the transcendental, *a priori* condition for all knowledge of the truth. In this context, Dooyeweerd speaks of our experiential horizon, which forms the transcendental framework within which human experience is alone possible; we are not able to look beyond that horizon.

This transcendental condition is not sufficient, however. The human Ego, the heart, as the religious root of all knowing-activity, is the *transcendent* condition for all knowledge of the truth. Because of this dimension, all knowledge of the truth is, in the deepest sense, of a transcendent-religious nature, be it in its orientation toward the God of the Scriptures, or be it in its apostate orientation toward the idols. It does not matter of what nature these idols are: images of gold and silver in primitive religions, or the idols of reason, observation, and science for many modern scientists, including quite a few theologians. Both in biblical and in apostate thinking, the transcendent-religious condition of the heart comprises, and at the same time transcends, the immanent experiential horizon.

Among the *a priori* elements of truth, we distinguish *a priori* elements both on the law-side and on the subject-side of the creational law-order. The structural *a priori* elements of practical and theoretical thought exhibit a lawful character; they do not belong on the subject-side but on the law-side of reality. Therefore, these *a priori* elements have to be distinguished from, for instance, the scientist's *insight* into the laws. This insight also forms an *a priori,* but one on the subject-side of the creational order. *A priori* elements on the law-side can never be right or wrong; they are simply divinely given. But *a priori* elements on the subject-side *can* be right or wrong, or a mixture of both.

In summary:

1. *True* knowledge, in the fullest sense of the word, with regard to cosmic reality is dependent upon *true*—explicit or implicit—knowledge of the structural *a priori* elements of all practical and theoretical knowledge.

2. Such a knowledge is itself dependent upon an explicitly or implicitly *true* insight into the transcendent condition of all practical and theoretical knowledge. This is an insight of the human heart as the transcendent-religious root of all thinking and knowing activity.

3. Such an insight is itself dependent upon a *true* knowledge, which we possess in our very hearts, with regard to God, who has revealed himself in Jesus Christ. In him is the transcendent fullness of the Truth, which shines through all practical and theoretical knowledge concerning our empirical creational reality.

Let me close with this word of Jesus (John 18:37): "For this purpose I was born and for this purpose I have come into the world—to bear witness to the truth. Everyone who is of the truth listens to my voice."

Questions for Review

1. Apply the ideas of structure and direction to the nature of true science and false science.

2. How would you distinguish between practical truth and theoretical truth?

3. What is logical positivism?

4. What is biblicistic negativism?

5. Briefly explain the following theories of truth:
    • the correspondence theory
    • the coherence theory
    • the pragmatic theory

6. What is scientific realism, and who held to this? And why?

7. What is instrumentalism, and who held to this? And why?

8. What is critical realism? What reasons did philosophers of science have to adopt this position?

9. Explain what it means to describe asocial or uneconomic conduct as being socially or economically false.

10. What is the difference between transcendental truth and transcendent truth?

11. On what three things is true knowledge dependent?

CONCISE BIBLIOGRAPHY

N.B. – I have included none of the numerous journal articles and book chapters on the Amsterdam school of philosophy.

Bril, K.A., Hart, H. & Klapwijk, J. (eds.). 1973. *The Idea of a Christian Philosophy: Essays in Honour of D.H.Th. Vollenhoven*. Toronto: Wedge.

Clouser, R.A. 1991, 2005. *The Myth of Religious Neutrality: An Essay on the Hidden Role of Religious Beliefs*. 2nd ed., Notre Dame: University of Notre Dame Press.

Clouser, R.A. 1999. *Knowing with the Heart: Religious Experience and Belief in God*. Eugene: Wipf & Stock.

Dooyeweerd, H. 1948. *Transcendental Problems of Philosophic Thought: An Inquiry into the Transcendental Conditions of Philosophy*. Eerdmans: Grand Rapids.

Dooyeweerd, H. 1960. *In the Twilight of Western Thought: Studies in the Pretended Autonomy of Philosophical Thought*. Philadelphia: Presbyterian & Reformed Publishing Company.

Dooyeweerd, H. 1968. *The Christian Idea of the State*. Nutley: The Craig Press.

Dooyeweerd, H. 1979, 2003 (repr.). *Roots of Western Culture: Pagan, Secular, and Christian Options*. Lewiston: Edwin Mellen Press.

Dooyeweerd, H. 1984 (repr.). *A New Critique of Theoretical Thought*, I: *The Necessary Presuppositions of Philosophy* (1953); II: *The General Theory of the Modal Spheres* (1955); III: *The Structures of Individuality of Temporal Reality* (1957). Jordan Station: Paideia Press.

Dooyeweerd, H. 1986. *A Christian Theory of Social Institutions*. Jordan Station: Paideia Press.

Dooyeweerd, H. 1997. *Collected Works of Herman Dooyeweerd* Series B, Vol. I: *Christian Philosophy and the Meaning of History*. Lewiston: Edwin Mellen Press.

Fernhout, H. 1975. *Man, Faith, and Religion in Bavinck, Kuyper, and Dooyeweerd*. Toronto: Institute for Christian Studies.

Griffioen, S. & Balk, B. (eds.). 1995. *Christian Philosophy at the Close of the Twentieth Century: Assessment and Perspective.* Kampen: Kok.

Hart, H. 1984. *Understanding our World: An Integral Ontology.* Lanham: University Press of America.

Hart, H., Van der Hoeven, J. & Wolterstorff, N. (eds.). 1983. *Rationality in the Calvinian Tradition.* Lanham: University Press of America.

Henderson, R.D. 1994. *Illuminating Law: The Construction of Herman Dooyeweerd's Philosophy 1918-1928.* Amsterdam: Buijten & Schipperheijn.

Kok, J.H. 1992. *Vollenhoven: His Early Development.* Sioux Center: Dordt College Press.

Kok, J.H. (ed.). 2004. *Ways of Knowing in Concert.* Sioux Center: Dordt College Press.

Kraay, J. & Tol, A. (eds.). 1979. *Hearing and Doing: Philosophical Essays dedicated to H. Evan Runner.* Toronto: Wedge.

McIntire, C.T. (ed.). 1985. *The Legacy of Herman Dooyeweerd: Reflections on Critical Philosophy in the Christian tradition.* Lanham: University Press of America.

Marshall, P., Griffioen, S. & Mouw, R. (eds.). 1989. *Stained Glass: Worldviews and Social Science.* Lanham: University Press of America.

Runner, H.E. 2009. *The Relation of the Bible to Learning.* Paideia Press.

Schuurman, E. 1987. *Christians in Babel.* Jordan Station: Paideia Press.

Schuurman, E. 1995. *The Technological Culture between the Times: A Christian Philosophical Assessment of Contemporary Society.* Sioux Center: Dordt College Press.

Spier, J.M. 1976. *An Introduction to Christian Philosophy.* Nutley: Craig Press.

Spykman, G.J. 1992. *Reformational Theology: A New Paradigm for Doing Dogmatics.* Grand Rapids: Eerdmans.

Stafleu, M.D. 1980. *Time and Again: A Systematic Analysis of the Foundations of Physics.* Toronto: Wedge/Bloemfontein: Sacum.

Stafleu, M.D. 1987. *Theories At Work: On the Structure and Functioning of Theories in Science, in Particular During the Copernican Revolution.* Lanham: University Press of America.

Strauss, D.F.M. 1991. *Man and his World.* Bloemfontein: Tekskor.

Strauss, D.F.M. 2009. *Philosophy: Discipline of the Disciplines.* Grand Rapids: Paideia Press.

Strauss, D.F.M. & Botting, M. (eds.). 2000. *Contemporary Reflections on the Philosophy of Herman Dooyeweerd.* Lewiston: Edwin Mellen Press.

Tol, A. 2010. *Philosophy in the Making: D.H.Th. Vollenhoven and the Emergence of Reformed Philosophy.* Sioux Center: Dordt College Press.

Troost, A. 1983. *The Christian Ethos: A Philosophical Survey.* Bloemfontein: Patmos.

Troost, A. 2012. *What Is Reformational Philosophy? An Introduction to the Cosmonomic Philosophy of Herman Dooyeweerd.* Grand Rapids: Paideia Press.

Truth and Reality: Philosophical Perspectives on Reality, Dedicated to Professor Dr. H.G. Stoker. 1971. Braamfontein: De Jong.

Van Riessen, H. 1965. *Christian Approach to Politics.* Amsterdam: Vrije Universiteit.

Van Riessen, H. 1966. *The Christian Approach to Science.* Hamilton: Association for Reformed Scientific Studies.

Wolters, A. 1975. *Our Place in the Philosophical Tradition.* Toronto: Institute for Christian Studies.

Wolters, A. 1986. *Creation Regained: A Transforming View of the World.* Leicester: Inter-Varsity Press.

SCRIPTURE INDEX

Genesis 1:26-28	70, 108, 109
Genesis 2:15	84
Genesis 2:19-20	177
Genesis 3	112, 119
Genesis 3:23	84
Genesis 4:1	32, 120
Genesis 4:15	110
Genesis 9:6	108, 110
Genesis 9:25	140
Exodus 18:21	175
Leviticus 25:8-55	151
Deuteronomy 5:11	140
Deuteronomy 32:8	140
Deuteronomy 33:14a	119
1 Samuel 9:9	18
Nehemiah 7:2	175
Job 9:8a	119
Job 25:5a	119
Job 26:7b	119
Job 37:14b	81
Job 38:33	59
Job 38-41	185
Psalms 31:5	175
Psalms 63:1	104
Psalms 119:89, 91	59
Psalms 148:6, 8	59
Proverbs 4:23	30
Proverbs 20:6b	175
Proverbs 30:23	124
Ecclesiastes 3:1-8	56

Ecclesiastes 9:9   109

Isaiah 28:24-26   176-177
Isaiah 40:12b   119
Isaiah 45:12   59

Jeremiah 10:10   175
Jeremiah 31:35   59
Jeremiah 33:25   59

Matthew 1:25   32
Matthew 4:45   77
Matthew 6:33   152
Matthew 26:11   140
Matthew 28:18-20   79

Mark 4:28   165

John 1:29   79
John 3:3-5   33
John 7:38-39   185
John 13:34   152
John 14:6   174, 185
John 14:17   185
John 15:26   185
John 16:13   161, 185
John 17:3   32, 120
John 17:17   174
John 18:37   174, 190

Acts 2   112
Acts 14:16   140
Acts 15:10   75

Romans 1:22-23   49
Romans 3:4, 7   175
Romans 5:5   152
Romans 8:3   76
Romans 10:14, 17   18
Romans 13   113
Romans 13:1-7   110-111
Romans 14:17   152

Romans 14:17-18   79

1 Corinthians 2:16   33
1 Corinthians 4:20   79
1 Corinthians 11:7   108
1 Corinthians 15:45, 47   70

2 Corinthians 4:4   108

Galatians 5:16-25   107

Ephesians 2:6   112
Ephesians 3:18   151
Ephesians 4:21   174
Ephesians 5:25, 28, 33   109

Philippians 4:8   152

Colossians 1:13   79
Colossians 1:15   108
Colossians 1:15-22   70
Colossians 1:16   185
Colossians 1:17a   119
Colossians 2:3   185
Colossians 2:8   185
Colossians 3:19   109

1 Thessalonians 5:23   103

2 Timothy 2:13   76

Titus 2:4   109
Titus 3:5   33

Hebrews 1:3   119
Hebrews 2:14   76
Hebrews 11:1   152

1 John 1:1-4   32
1 John 3:19   174

Revelation 4:11   59

SUBJECT INDEX

Absolutism, 47-49, 107, 145, 147
Adler, Alfred, 147, 182
Althaus, Paul, 159
Atheism, 11-12, 35, 138, 142, 145, 151, 157, 166-167
Analogies, 55, 72-74, 138
Analytical philosophy, 13, 158, 162
Animals, 31, 49, 52, 59-60, 67, 69-71, 81, 86-88, 92, 97, 102, 108, 122, 130, 138, 177
      Higher, 66, 82-83, 93-95, 97-100
      Lower, 66, 82, 92-93
Apologetics, 33
Aquinas, Thomas, 22-23
Aristotle, 19, 82, 144, 180-181
Augustine, 22, 54
Aulén, Gustav, 159

Bacon, Francis, 133
Beliefs, 8-11, 13-15, 20, 22-26, 28, 30-34, 43, 51, 59, 64, 66, 68, 72, 102, 109, 113, 118, 124, 137-139, 142-146, 150, 152, 164, 168-169, 174, 180, 188
Bellarmine, Roberto, 181
Bergson, Henri, 182
Berkeley, George, 48, 181
Beza, Theodore, 24
Biblicism, 150, 158, 160-161, 170, 176
Body, 98, 103-105
Bonaventura, 165-166
Boyle, Robert, 20
Brunner, Emil, 159

Calvin, John, 24, 76, 165
Capra, Fritjof, 28
Caputo, John D., 164-165
Chomsky, Noam, 141, 148
Christian anthropology, 107-108
Church, 10, 52, 89, 110-114, 138, 141, 151
Copernicus, Nicolaus, 20, 181
Cosmic reality, 5-6, 20, 39-58, 59-79, 81-82, 84, 88, 90-92, 98, 102-103, 105, 107, 109, 112, 117, 122, 126-127, 129, 134, 137, 142, 144, 149-150, 152,

156-157, 174, 176, 180, 184-186, 189-190. See also Cosmology.
    Factual side, 60-61, 71-72, 75, 134
    Law-side, 60-61, 71-72, 75, 134, 152
Cosmology, 5-8, 39, 162, 170. See also Metaphysics, Ontology, Reality
Creation, 34-35, 49-50, 53, 62-65, 70-71, 75-79, 84, 106, 110, 114, 140, 150-152, 176-177, 182, 185-186, 190
Culture, 3-5, 47-49, 78-79, 84-86, 88-90, 109-110, 118, 138-140, 146, 156, 164, 176-177
    Cultural mandate, 78, 85

Davies, Paul, 146. See also Naturalism
De Boer, Theo, 169
Defining, means of, 82
Dennett, Daniel, 141-142
Descartes, Réne, 47, 87
Determinism, 13
Direction, 76-77, 166-167, 170. See also Vollenhoven, Dirk
Dooyeweerd, Herman, 26-27, 30, 34-35, 40-41, 46, 50, 52-54, 59, 75, 87-89, 100, 102, 128, 159, 164-166, 169-170, 189. See also Ground-motive.
    Law-spheres, 59-79
Dualism, 50, 103-107, 181

Ebeling, Gerhard, 158
Ego, 9-10, 30, 102-106, 189. See also Heart
Einstein, Albert, 25, 54, 182
Enlightenment, the, 24, 29, 34, 118, 160-161
Entity, 81-83, 85-88, 91-94, 98-99, 104, 133, 170, 187. See also Idionomy
    Destination function, 87, 109-114
    Foundational function, 87-95, 98-99, 101, 109-112
    Qualifying function, 83, 87
    Typical function, 88
Epistemology, 5, 7-8, 39, 43-44, 51, 65, 67, 162, 174, 189
Erickson, Millard J., 160
Evolutionism, 29, 34, 46-47, 109, 145, 147
Existentialism, 13, 28, 158, 162, 182. See also Heidegger, Martin; Sartre, Jean-Paul

Faith, 8-15, 21, 23-34, 43, 50, 64, 73-74, 79, 102, 108, 117-119, 126, 131-132, 137, 142-144, 147, 151-153, 155, 161-163, 174, 181, 185-188
Family, 109-111, 113-114, 141, 151
Faraday, Michael, 182
Friedman, Milton, 148

Friendship, 110
Freud, Sigmund, 25, 27, 48, 145, 147, 182

Galilei, Galileo, 20, 47, 144, 181
Geisler, Norman L., 163, 180
Gray, John, 141
Ground-motive, 8, 27, 34-35, 137-138, 140, 162, 164-170. See also Dooyeweerd, Herman.

Habermas, Jürgen, 141
Hart, Hendrik, 60, 170
Hawking, Stephen, 146. See also Naturalism
Heart, 12, 24, 27, 30-35, 77-79, 100, 103-108, 131, 137-138, 142-143, 149, 152, 161-162, 166, 169, 180, 186-187, 189-190. See also Ego
Hegel, Georg W.F., 35
Heidegger, Martin, 28, 182. See also Existentialism
Heraclitus, 19, 48
Hermeneutical circle, 167-168
Hesiod, 19
Holmes, Arthur F., 176
Homer, 19
Human existence, 28, 97-98, 105, 107
        Corporeality, 97-98, 100, 102, 104, 106, 147
Humanism, 34-35, 145, 147, 158, 163-168, 170

Idionomy, 86-95, 97-102, 105, 107, 129. See also Entity
        Biotic, 89, 91-94, 97-100, 104-105
        Encapsis, 88-92, 95
        Energetic, 89-94, 97-98, 100
        Perceptive, 92-94, 97-100, 104
        Sensitive, 94, 97-100, 104
        Spiritive, 97-102, 104-105
Idolatry, 48-51, 68, 70, 77-78, 108, 114, 142-143, 189
Immanence, 30-31, 98, 102-108, 112-113, 138, 142, 148, 162, 170, 174-175, 189
Instrumentalism, 180-184

Jacob, François, 147
Jung, Carl G., 147, 182

Kant, Immanuel, 6, 24, 48, 155, 164
Kepler, Johannes, 20
Keynes, John Maynard, 148

Kierkegaard, Søren, 35
Knowledge, 5-6, 17-19, 31-33, 44, 69, 81, 107-108, 117-125, 128-130, 132, 139, 151, 155-157, 161-162, 174, 185, 189-190
      Practical, 2, 117, 119-125, 129, 131-132, 175-176, 178, 180, 185-190
      Theoretical, 2, 5, 19, 117, 119-125, 131-132, 175, 178, 180, 185-190
Kuhn, Thomas, 25, 28
Kuyper, Abraham, 52-53, 85, 165

Lakatos, Imre, 25, 28
Language, 15, 17, 130-131, 134, 148, 150, 163
Law, 33, 53, 59-79, 86-87, 126-127, 129, 133-134, 152, 174, 176, 184, 190
      As boundary, 74-76, 152
      Law-order (natural laws), 20, 59-66, 69-71, 74, 77-79, 134, 150, 152, 156, 174, 176-177, 184, 189-190
Lessing, Theodor, 148
Luther, Martin, 24, 159
Lyotard, Jean-François, 29, 139. See also Postmodernism

MacIntyre, Alasdair, 8
Marriage, 52, 109-111, 113-114, 122, 132, 151
Marx, Karl, 48, 148
Marxism, 47, 50, 145
Maslow, Abraham, 147
Materialism (physicalism), 12, 15, 33-34, 47, 49-50, 91, 109, 138, 141, 145, 151, 157
Maxwell, James Clerk, 182
Melanchthon, Philipp, 24
Metaphysical realism, 163
Metaphysics, 5-6. See also Cosmology, Ontology
Michelangelo, 85-86
Mind, 3, 41, 47, 97-98, 100-102. See also Spirit
Modal aspects, 44-57, 59-61, 64-74, 76, 81-85, 87-88, 90-92, 94-95, 100-103, 109-113, 123-128, 137-138, 147, 149, 170, 185, 187. See also Reality
      Aesthetic, 43, 45, 48, 51, 56, 63-65, 67-68, 72-74, 85-88, 97, 99, 101, 109, 114, 121, 123, 126, 149, 151-152, 185, 188-189
      Arithmetical, 40-45, 47, 49, 51, 54-55, 61, 64, 66, 68, 71, 83, 128
      Biotic, 39-47, 50-52, 55, 61, 63, 65-68, 71, 74, 83, 85, 109-110, 123, 127, 132, 185, 187
      Economic, 39, 43, 45, 47-52, 56, 61-65, 67-69, 71-74, 86-88, 97, 101, 109, 111-112, 114, 123, 127, 148-149, 151
      Energetic, 40-45, 47, 49-50, 55, 65-66, 68, 71-74, 83, 85, 87, 138
      Ethical, 39, 43-46, 48, 50-51, 56, 62-65, 68, 72-73, 86-88, 97, 99-102,

110-114, 123, 127-128, 149
Formative (Historical), 42-45, 48, 51-52, 56, 62, 64, 67-69, 73-74, 85-86, 88, 97, 100-101, 109-112, 114, 139-140
Juridical, 43, 45, 50-51, 56, 62, 64, 67-69, 72-73, 86, 97, 99, 101-102, 109-112, 114, 123, 132, 152, 187
Kinematic, 40-45, 47, 54, 55, 64, 66, 68, 71, 74, 83, 138
Lingual, 39, 42-43, 45, 48, 56, 62, 64, 67-69, 72-74, 77, 86, 97, 100-101, 109-110, 112, 114, 150
Logical, 41-43, 45, 48-51, 56, 61-65, 67-69, 71-74, 83, 86, 97, 100-101, 109, 112, 114, 126-127, 138-139, 149-150, 188
Perceptive, 41-45, 48, 55, 66, 68, 83, 126
Pistical, 43-45, 48, 50-51, 53, 56-57, 62-64, 68-69, 72-74, 83-84, 86, 97, 101-103, 109, 112-114, 126, 131, 142-143, 149, 152, 156, 185, 187
Sensitive, 41-43, 45-46, 48, 50, 56, 66-68, 72-74, 82-83, 88, 109, 123, 126-127, 137-138, 188
Social, 42-48, 50-52, 56, 62-64, 66-69, 73-74, 85-87, 90, 97, 101, 109-112, 114, 123, 127, 140-142, 148-151
Spatial, 40-45, 47, 51, 55, 61, 66, 68, 71, 74, 83, 87
Mysticism, 28, 106, 160-161

Naturalism, 146-147
Nature, 3, 19-20, 29, 34, 77-78, 84-85, 122-123, 131, 156, 176, 181-182
Neo-Kantianism, 164
Neo-Platonism, 169
New Age movement, 28-29, 34
Newton, Isaac, 20, 181-182
Niebuhr, Reinhold, 35
Nietzsche, Friedrich, 182
Nihilism, 11-12, 15, 141, 143, 151
Nussbaum, Martha, 141-142

Object-function, 65-71, 83-86, 91-93, 108, 185
Objectivism, 13
Occam, William of: see William of Occam
Ontology, 5, 39, 43-44, 51, 65, 174, 189. See also Metaphysics, Cosmology
Osiander, Andreas, 181
Ott, Heinrich, 158

Parmenides, 19
Pascal, Blaise, 24
Pasteur, Louis, 182
Phenomenology, 162

Philosophical Anthropology, 3, 9, 25, 104, 107-108
Philosophy. See also Epistemology, Ethics, Ontology, Wisdom
    is "seeing," 17-21
    is "thinking," 17-21, 25
    Christian Philosophy, 1-2, 12-15, 20-22, 25-26, 28, 39, 50-51, 55,
        59, 63, 65, 69-76, 84-85, 89, 100, 106, 112, 117, 120-123, 129, 131-
        132, 149, 155-170, 173-175, 184-187
    Definition of, 1-4, 6-7, 17
    in Ancient Greece, 19-22, 34, 103-105, 144-145, 163, 165
    in Early Christianity, 21-23
    in the Middle Ages, 21-23, 34, 103, 158
    in the Modern Age, 23-24, 163
    in the Twentieth Century, 25-26
Plato, 19, 81-82, 173, 180-181
Polanyi, Michael, 25
Popper, Karl, 25, 28, 60, 133, 177-178
Positivism, 13, 118-119, 121, 129, 158-159, 175-176
Postmodernism, 13, 29, 34, 118, 139, 158, 164, 173. See also Jean-François
    Lyotard.
Pragmatism, 162
Prolegomena (Premises), 157-158, 162-164, 166-167
Psychoanalysis, 182
Putnam, Hilary, 168
Pythagoras, 47, 61

Radical historicism, 182
Rationalism, 12, 24-25, 47, 49-50, 107, 118, 121, 123, 130, 132, 145, 149, 159-
    161, 168-169, 180
Realism, 180-184
Reason, 9-12, 21-33, 47-48, 76, 105-107, 118-120, 137-138, 142-146, 150, 155-
    156, 158-159, 161-162, 181, 189. See also Rationalism.
Reductionism, 47-50, 94, 97, 100-101, 147, 151
Reformation, the, 23-24, 103, 111, 165
Relationships, 9, 43, 47-48, 51, 56, 62, 68, 77, 108-114, 121, 138-139, 141,
    151. See also Marriage, Family, Friendship, State, Church
Relativism, 11, 173
Religion, 7-8, 10-15, 19, 24, 26, 27-29, 31, 48, 50, 105-108, 113, 117, 125-126,
    138, 141-143, 146, 173, 189-190
Ricoeur, Paul, 35
Runner, H. Evan, 26

Sartre, Jean-Paul, 28, 182. See also Existentialism

Schaeffer, Francis, 7-8
Schelling, Friedrich W.J., 35
Scholasticism, 34, 76, 103-107, 158, 160-163, 165-168, 170, 181
Schopenhauer, Arthur, 182
Schweitzer, Albert, 35
Science, 1-7, 9-10, 14-15, 17-29, 31-33, 39-47, 49, 59-60, 73, 77-79, 84, 104,
    106, 117-134, 137-139, 143-149, 152-153, 155-159, 161-163, 165-167, 174-
    182, 184-190
      and Abstraction, 126-128
      Aesthetics, 6, 43, 45, 63, 125-127, 188
      Biology, 1, 4, 19, 39-42, 44-46, 122-123, 127, 131-132, 149
      Deduction, 134
      Economics, 1, 4, 6, 39, 45, 48-49, 67, 122, 127, 148, 151, 187
      Ethics, 6, 43-45, 48, 156, 188
      Formative sciences, 42, 44-45
      History, 42, 148-150, 157
      Humanities, 1, 4, 6, 41-42, 102, 125, 127, 147-149
      Induction, 134
      Jurisprudence (Justice), 43, 46, 50-52, 56, 67, 111, 127, 149, 188
      Linguistics, 4, 9, 31, 39, 42-43, 45, 48, 49, 67, 77, 148, 150
      Logic, 9-10, 21, 41-42, 45, 47-49, 60, 62, 134
      Mathematics, 1-4, 19, 22, 33, 39-41, 43-45, 49, 128, 134, 181
      Observation, 128-129, 131-133
      Physics, 3, 19, 25, 28, 39-41, 44-46, 49, 54, 91, 93-94, 97-100, 121,
        126, 128, 132, 146-147, 182
      Psychology, 1-5, 19, 25, 27, 40-42, 45, 48, 102, 117, 123, 125-126,
        132, 147, 149, 156
      Sociology, 1, 4, 6, 42-46, 127, 156,
Scientism, 117, 120, 132, 180
      Biblioscientism, 118-119, 131
Secularization, 24, 117-118, 144-145
Sen, Amartya, 141
Sin, 71, 76-79, 106-107, 151, 158, 186
Skepticism, 173
Skinner, B. F., 147
Sloterdijk, Peter, 141
Solipsism, 11-12, 143, 151
Spengler, Oswald, 148
Sphere-sovereignty, 52-53, 111, 113. See also Kuyper, Abraham
Spirit (soul), 41, 98, 103-105, 107. See also Mind
Spykman, Gordon, 104, 164
State, 48, 52, 89, 110-114, 141, 148, 151

Stoker, Hendrik G., 26
Structure, 75-77, 170, See also Vollenhoven
Subject-function, 65-71, 81, 83-87, 91-92, 108
Supernaturalism, 146-147, 163

Taylor, Charles, 8, 141-142
Theism, 163
Theology, 1, 4, 21-23, 35, 43, 45, 53-54, 103, 106, 112, 117-118, 120, 125, 132, 149, 151, 155-170, 175-176, 179, 181, 187-189
Theory, Definition of, 17, 120, 128, 177-178, 182-184
Thielicke, Helmut, 159
Tillich, Paul, 159
Time, 53-57, 113, 162
        and God, 53-54
        and modalities, 54-57
        Cosmic, 55-57
Transcendence, 9-10, 30, 35, 102-108, 112-113, 138, 142, 147-150, 155-156, 162, 170, 174-175, 185-186, 189-190
Trillhaas, Wolfgang, 159
Troost, Andree, 26, 67, 159
Truth, 14, 22, 29, 131, 149, 169, 173-176, 178-182, 184-190
        Coherence Theory, 178-179, 184, 187
        Correspondence Theory, 178-180, 187

Utilitarianism, 13

Van Riessen, Hendrik, 26, 126
Verburg, Peit, 87
Vitalism, 182
Vollenhoven, Dirk, 26, 41, 76, 84, 159, 165-166, 170. See also Direction, Structure

Watson, John B., 147
Weber, Otto, 158-159
Weinberg, Steven, 146. See also Naturalism
William of Occam, 23
Wisdom, 17-19, 21, 139
Wittgenstein, Ludwig, 166
Worldview, 7-8, 12, 15, 22, 29, 31, 132, 137-153, 159, 177, 184, 188